Steps Towards
Educational Excellence

Steps Towards
Educational Excellence

The Role of Parents, Students and Supplementary Schools

GILBERT GBEDAWO

Copyright © 2015 by Gilbert Gbedawo.

Library of Congress Control Number:		2015912575
ISBN:	Hardcover	978-1-5144-6143-3
	Softcover	978-1-5144-6144-0
	eBook	978-1-5144-6145-7

All rights reserved. No part of this book may be reproduced or transmitted in any form or by any means, electronic or mechanical, including photocopying, recording, or by any information storage and retrieval system, without permission in writing from the copyright owner.

Any people depicted in stock imagery provided by Thinkstock are models, and such images are being used for illustrative purposes only.
Certain stock imagery © Thinkstock.

Print information available on the last page.

Rev. date: 09/07/2015

To order additional copies of this book, contact:
Xlibris
800-056-3182
www.Xlibrispublishing.co.uk
Orders@Xlibrispublishing.co.uk
705888

CONTENTS

Acknowledgements xiii

Abbreviations xv

Introduction xvii

Chapter 1   Migrant Children in Schools 1
    1.1   Introduction 1
    1.2   Background to the Study 2
    1.3   Structure 3
    1.4   Research Questions 3
    1.5   Significance of the Study 3
    1.6   Conclusion 4

Chapter 2   Review of the Literature 5
    2.1   Introduction 5
    2.2   Reasons for Achievement Gaps in Educational
          Attainment 5
    2.2.1   The Gap in Achievement 9
    2.3   Why Do Black Migrant Children Underachieve? 17
    2.4   The Role and Contributions of
          Supplementary Schools 20
    2.5   Supplementary Schools and Attainment 24
    2.6   Conclusion 26

Chapter 3   Methods and Methodology 27
    3.1   Introduction 27
    3.2   Human Capital Theory (HCT) 27
    3.3   Social Capital Theory 29
    3.4   Research Context 31
    3.5   Research Design and Strategy 32
    3.6   Interviewing 33
    3.7   Disadvantages of Interviewing 34

3.8	Complexities of Methodology	35
3.9	Document Analysis	37
3.10	Interpreting the Data	39
3.11	Validation of Findings	40
3.12	Limitation of the Study	41
3.13	Ethical Consideration	41
3.14	Conclusion	43
Chapter 4	Finding of the Study	44
4.1	Introduction	44
4.2	Application of the HCT to the Supplementary School	45
4.3	Application of the Social Capital Theory to the Supplementary School	51
4. 4	Parental Engagement and Social Capital Theory	55
4.5	Conclusion	61
Chapter 5	Conclusions and Recommendations	63
5.1	Introduction	63
5.2	Summary	63
5.3	Research Questions Revisited	65
5. 4	Research Findings	65
5.5	Conclusion	66
Chapter 6	The Role of Students towards Educational Excellence	68
Chapter 7	Seven Predictable Behaviours of Outstanding Students	77
Chapter 8	How to Maximise Learning	96
Chapter 9	Charity Begins at Home: Role of Parents	103
Chapter 10	Getting to Know Your Child	139
Appendices		179
References		191
Index		197

To my wife, Felicia and our three children, Prince Kekeli, Isabella and Gabriella for their love and patience.

This book is dedicated to the Holy Spirit who is my source of inner strength, senior mentor, counsellor, greatest teacher, and comforter. Thank you for guiding me always. Secondly, I would like to dedicate this to my daddy, Mr Gabriel H. A. Gbedawo, and to the loving memory of my precious mother, Esther who has since gone on to eternity.

I also dedicate this to Mr Anthony Ahiable and my wonderful aunties, Rose Asinyo Gbedawo, Christiana Avornyo, and Josephine Seshie Ati for their unflinching support and to my godfather Anthony Atitso Avornyo, who is now resting in eternity. To the family of Mr and Mrs Fraser and their children Izabel, Michael and Alice and to the branch pastor of KICC Romford minister Bimbo Odunsi and Princess Odunsi and all the family for their love and generosity. To the gracious Avornyo family, Seshie family, and Mr Richard Ekem family and to my amazing in-laws, Mr Geoffrey Eduam Yarney, the former headmaster of Winneba Secondary School and Mrs Theodora Yarney. Finally, to Mr Samuel and Mrs Violet Danso, Mrs Yemisi Akindele and the family, and all of my students past, present, and future.

All scriptures are taken from the King James Version of the Holy Bible unless otherwise stated.

And wisdom and knowledge shall be the stability of thy times, and strength of salvation: the fear of the LORD is his treasure. (Isaiah 33:6)

ACKNOWLEDGEMENTS

Firstly, I would like to thank the almighty God, who is the source of all wisdom and knowledge, and his son, Jesus Christ, my saviour and lord. Secondly, I would like to thank Dr Moses Oketch for his intellectual support and guidance during my time at the Institute of Education (IOE). Thirdly, I would like to express my thanks to Prof. Heidi Safia Mirza and all those who have taught me at IOE and Chris Yates. Fourthly, I would like to thank the leadership of St Matthew Academy in Blackheath for their financial support.

Thanks also to Mr Kwame Ocloo and the members of the Youth Learning Network for the gift of access and their immense support. Thanks to all parents, volunteers, and students of Synergy Education, especially Helena, Marlene, Akwasi and Tim. I would also like to appreciate Izabel Miti-Fraser and Michael Fraser for proofreading and editing the final draft of this book prior to publication. Thanks to Marlene Grant for typing my handwritten drafts, Gladys Ceniza for her commitment to see the work published, and my friends Alfred Kotey, Dr Gyamfi and the family, Rev De Lawrence, Charles FizzM, Matilda Dzomeku, Daniel Abavare and Christian Akpanya, Major Elikem Fiamavle, Afeti Fiamavle and Martine Conelle and the family.

I would also like to thank our senior pastor, Mathew Ashimolowo, and his wife, Pastor Yemisi Ashimolowo, of Kingsway International Christian Centre for pouring their lives into us by teaching us the word of God and for their ministry and prayers. I would like to express my sincere gratitude to Dr Mike Murdock for inspiring us to document our convictions and for proclaiming and publishing the wisdom of God.

Thanks to pastor Dipo Oluyomi, pastor Ade D'Almeida, pastor Esther Dunmoye, and all the ministers of KICC, especially John and Evelyn Egbenegbor, Dayo and Taiwo Ogundayo, Abimbola and Princess Odunsi, Gbenga Fashanu, Kayode Falebita and pastor Sam Appiah-Adu, Mr and Mrs Quansah. Thanks to minister Cecelia Anderson, Camilla Shittu, and all the deacons of KICC. Thanks to Mama Toks and all the members of the guest management team of KICC, especially sister Edith Ifekwuna and minister Bimbo Sagbola. Thanks to Mr and Mrs Daniel Suppey, Michael Dayo and Irene Agunbiade, and the entire KICC family, especially the Romford Chapel members. Thanks to Clement and Linda Chinengundu, Kenny and Tokunbo Akinwunmi, Obi and Eva Nwosa, Akwasi and Evelyn Asianowa, Mr and Mrs Bolaji Awoade, Irene and Gbenga Obadagbonyi, Daniel and Abiola Fakayode, Chijoke and Peace Ani and Fred Essienyi.

Thanks also to the pastors of ICGC in Ghana especially William Benito Okoro of Winneba and Anthony Dogbe of Aflao. Thank you for your prayers and tenacity. I would also like to acknowledge all my teachers at Winneba Secondary School, especially Mr Godfred Mensah, Mr Yawson and Mr Akoto, and all the teachers and past students of St Pauls Secondary School (SPACO).

I have completed this book through your immense prayers and support, and for this, I am grateful. Finally, thanks to all my brothers, Senanu for reading the manuscript and for your encouragement, Senyo, Selorm, Eli, and Joshua Gbedawo, my special nieces, Patience Avornyo, Chealsea Boamah and my dear cousins Rejoice and Eli Ati, Mr Gilbert Avornyo, Dr Anthony Avornyo and Colonel D. D. Gbedawo, his wife, Mrs Charity Gbedawo and David Dzifa Kemetse.

ABBREVIATIONS

YLN: Youth Learning Network

HCT: Human Capital Theory

SCT: Social Capital Theory

DFE: Department for Education

DCSF: Department for Children, Schools, and Families

DfES: Department for Education and Schools

OECD: Organisation for Economic Co-Operation and Development

KICC: Kingsway International Christian Centre

ICGC: International Central Gospel Church

INTRODUCTION

Minority ethnic communities in the United Kingdom have generated supplementary schools in response to perceived racial discriminations and prejudice confronting their children's educational development and attainment in mainstream schools. They formed supplementary schools to help restore the confidence and self-esteem of black children who are sometimes perceived as victims of institutional racism. However, the works of supplementary schools keep evolving just like those who participate in them.

Supplementary schools are also regarded by black parents as sites where educational gaps between the minorities and the majority white population can be closed, and so black parents enrol their children in them with the view to promote educational excellence. This qualitative case study of one such school seeks to find out how it contributes to the educational attainment of migrant children from other parts of the world who attend mainstream secondary schools.

The study found out that due to their very nature of being community-led, with small class sizes, dedicated and committed teachers who share similar cultural background as the students, higher parental involvements, strong leadership, and several other initiatives, supplementary schools can and are making positive contributions to the educational attainment of migrant children.

The study also found that the experiences of the students who participate in supplementary schools and, indeed, the teachers and parents are positive, positioning supplementary schools as sites for the effective engagement of learners from migrant communities, especially those who are disengaged in mainstream setting.

The second part of this book focuses on what students can do to achieve educational success and how parental support can facilitate excellent educational outcomes for children. The book covers areas such as the seven predictable behaviours of outstanding students, how to maximise learning, seven decisions that guarantee successful homes, and seven things every parent should know about their children to unleash their potential as learners.

CHAPTER 1

Migrant Children in Schools

1.1 Introduction

The central aim of this book is to find out how supplementary schools are contributing to the educational attainment of migrant children in UK secondary schools and the roles of students and parents in attaining educational excellence. Migration is not a new phenomenon but it has always been part and parcel of civilisation itself. However, the recent events of migration of people of African descent and those whose countries have been ravaged by armed conflict have once again dominated the news. We have seen the devastating consequences of migrants trying to cross the Atlantic Ocean to find peaceful habitation in the nations of Europe. Some of these migrants have died on the journey to reach the shores of Europe, and others have survived these perilous journeys partly due to the rescue operations of the governments of Italy and recently the United Kingdom.

The reasons for the migration are sometimes economic, social, religious, or political in nature. The fates of these migrants, especially the children and young people, will be determined by the experiences they have in the educational systems of their host nations, but like many before them, this book seeks to understand their experiences and give insight into how supplementary education and parents enhance the educational aspirations of the migrant children by positioning them towards a life of success in their new homes.

This chapter gives a brief overview of migrant children in the UK, the structure of the book, research questions, significance of the study, and conclusion.

1.2 Background to the Study

The growth in the population of migrants subsequently resulted in the growth of the population of migrant children in UK schools. Reynolds (2008) recalled that 'in 2005 the Office of National Statistics (ONS) stated that 32,000 children arrived from overseas moved to live in the UK and under Article 28 of the United Nations Convention on the rights of the Child (UN 1989) and Article 2 of the first protocol of the European Convention on Human Rights (EU 1998), both of which the UK is signatory to, all states must recognise the right of every child to an education'. Reynolds (2008) hence reiterated that 'UK schools must absorb these migrant children into their student populations'. Despite the growth in the population of migrant children in UK secondary schools, it is noted that this is a largely unresearched area (Ackers and Stalford; Anderson and O'Connell Davidson 2008). Lentin (2008: 116) noted that 'since the end of the 1990s, voices have increasingly been heard decrying a crisis in multiculturalism or the failure of integration in societies of immigration. This can be witnessed in the attack on affirmative action in the United States, the criminalization of immigration in Europe, the change of citizenship criteria and ceremonies in several countries, the rise of Islam phobia, the rolling back of civil liberties as a fallout of the "War on Terror" and the increased recourse to racial and ethnic profiling in the service of greater national security.' The surge in the population of migrant children into secondary schools in the UK, like the events stated above, have and will continue to be surrounded by controversy and suspicion. While some may regard it as problematic (Clark et al.; 1999), others think that it fosters and promotes integration (Goodson and Phillimore 2008).

1.3 Structure

Chapter 1 focuses on the background to the study, research questions, significance of the study, and conclusion. Chapter 2 reviews the relevant literature based on the research questions. In chapter 3, the research methods and methodology are presented. Chapter 4 then presents the findings based on the research questions, and chapter 5 of the book summarises the key findings and presents the recommendations. Chapter 6 examines the role of students towards educational excellence. Chapter 7 deals with the seven predictable behaviours of outstanding students. Chapter 8 discusses how students can maximise learning. Chapter 9 focuses on the role of parents and chapter 10 concludes the book with the importance of knowing and placing value on your child.

1.4 Research Questions

My main research questions are:

1. What are the experiences of migrant children in UK supplementary schools in relation to mainstream secondary schools?
2. How are supplementary schools contributing to the educational attainment of migrant students during GCSE secondary school examination?
3. How are migrant parents involved in supplementary schools?
4. What are the roles of students and parents in ensuring educational excellence and success?

1.5 Significance of the Study

Due to cultural differences and sometimes linguistic issues, mainstream schools often struggle to meet the specific needs of black minority ethnic children and, most especially, new migrant children from Africa. Most of the time, this leads to negative outcomes for the different stakeholders in the schools where the children attend. Consequently, parents send their children to supplementary schools as a means to address the perceived racial prejudice and discrimination their children suffer in mainstream school. Although supplementary schools for blacks have been in existence for over four decades, little is written or known about their impact on the educational attainment of migrant children. Through this study, I set out to investigate why they existed, how they contribute to the educational outcome of migrant children from Africa in UK secondary schools, and the experiences of the students who attend them. This study can then help all the stakeholders in education to discover the contributions of supplementary schools and can also help to forge a positive and engaging relationship between mainstream schools and supplementary school as a way of tackling the underachievement often associated with migrant students.

1.6 Conclusion

This chapter has provided the background to the study in detail and outlined the structure of the study. It also listed the research questions and, finally, identified the significance of the study.

CHAPTER 2

Review of the Literature

2.1 Introduction

The chapter examines the various debates about the underachievement of migrant children and the reasons why some of them fail to achieve in mainstream setting. It also examines the rationale for setting up supplementary schools and their perceived benefits.

2.2 Reasons for Achievement Gaps in Educational Attainment

Owen et al, (2000), gave the following account of the demographic nature of minority ethnic groups in the UK. The minority ethnic group population of Great Britain has grown continuously since the late 1940s. It reached more than 1 million in the late 1960s and 3 million by 1991, and it has continued to grow rapidly to over 3.8 million in 1999. Minority ethnic groups are projected to account for more than half of the growth in the working-age population over the next ten years. This rapid growth is a consequence of relatively large numbers of births in the UK due to the very youthful age structure of most minority ethnic groups and the continued immigration of people from particular ethnic groups.

The bulk of the minority population is from South Asian ethnic groups, with Indians being the largest single ethnic group. The black African and Bangladeshi ethnic groups are two of the most rapidly growing. Minority ethnic groups form a much larger percentage of children and young people than they do of older people. They account for an increasing percentage of new entrants to the labour market since the number of young adults in the white population declined sharply during the 1990s.

In an article published in the Daily Times on 5th May 2014, James Chapman noted that 'Britain's black and ethnic minority communities could account for almost a third of the population by 2050, according to a report published today. The number of people from minority groups could as much as double by then, it says.

One in four children under the age of ten in the UK is already from a minority group and over the next few decades the proportion will soar, according to think-tank Policy Exchange.

Currently, eight million people, or 14 per cent of the UK population, are from ethnic minorities. But they now account for 80 per cent of population growth, while the white population remains constant.

Experts predict that as a result, by the middle of the century between 20 per cent and 30 per cent of the population – up to 16million people – will be from a minority community, the report says'.

(http://www.dailymail.co.uk/news/ article-2620957/Ethnic-minorities)

But how has this numerical growth compared to their educational attainment in schools? Owen et al. (2000) , made the following observation on the examination performance of minority ethnic pupils compared to their white counterparts: 'The level of achievement in the GCSE examination steadily improved during the 1990s across all ethnic groups.'

However, there are still wide gaps in attainment between ethnic groups. Data for the period of 1994 to 1997 show that Indian students are most likely to achieve five or more passes at GCSE grades A* to C. Black and Pakistani or Bangladeshi students display the lowest levels of achievement. White students perform better than those from minority ethnic groups overall, but fewer achieved five or more passes at GCSE grades A* to C than those from Indian and other ethnic groups. Across all ethnic groups, students whose fathers worked in managerial and professional jobs are most likely to do well in their GCSE examinations, and those whose fathers were in manual occupations fare worst. Students attending independent and grant-maintained schools were also more likely than those attending LEA-controlled schools to achieve good results in their GCSE examinations in 1996/7.

Does this indicate that parental occupation determines the educational attainment of students? What about the type of school one attends? Are these important indicators of educational attainment in schools? Owen et al. (2000), however, noted from a recent research data that 'the experience of minority ethnic groups is not uniform, and that the accepted picture of minority disadvantage ignores the evidence of considerable progress and achievement by people from minority ethnic groups in examination results, job creation and career progression'. However, Kendall et al. (2005), made the observation in the summary of their research report findings that, overall, pupils from minority ethnic groups are more likely than those from white UK backgrounds to live in low-income households. This is more evident for some ethnic groups than for others for example, almost two-thirds of Pakistani and Bangladeshi households and about a quarter of black households are classified as having low income. There are substantial differences between ethnic groups in terms of levels of attainment. Pupils from Chinese and Indian backgrounds generally have relatively high levels of attainment, while those from black African, Bangladeshi, and Pakistani backgrounds achieve below the national average. The question then is, how does your socio-economic status play out in the educational outcome? Kendall et al, (2005), went further to report that black African pupils also had lower levels of attainment than pupils from white UK backgrounds at key stages 2 and 3. However, during key stage 4, pupils from black African background made relatively good progress, and by the end of key stage 4, their attainment was similar to that of white UK pupils in the Excellence in Cities phase 1 areas and slightly below that of white UK pupils in non–Excellence in Cities areas. I would like to know how they managed to close the gap in this situation. Do you want to find out too?

A major characteristic of these black African students is that 40 per cent of them are on free school meal, which is an indicator of poverty and deprivation. It is possible to reason that this deprivation and poverty to some extent affects negatively the educational outcomes of these pupils. The OECD Working Party on Migration (1983), agrees that 'the home and social environment and the de facto status of many of them (migrant children) do not encourage them to profit fully from the education and training they might receive'. The report stated further that the causes of failure of migrant children in school based on research illuminated a whole range of different factors, such as inadequate knowledge of the teaching language, socio-economic characteristics of first and second generation migrants, and their attitudes towards the institution of education. In a report by the Commission of the European Communities (2009) on the children of migrant workers, it was found that the problems and difficulties encountered by migrant children are similar to those encountered by children from poorer backgrounds. Migrant children do not find suitable material conditions for working at home or a lifestyle and atmosphere likely to encourage their development in the educational environment of the school. The distance between the migrant child and the indigenous child is accentuated by the parents' failure to integrate and by the fact that the school in the host country is not geared to his or her needs. Most children coming from migrant backgrounds have significantly lower levels of educational attainment, often resulting in their early-school leaving , low qualifications level and lack of participation in higher education. Children who do not only face linguistic and cultural barriers, but who also suffer from poor socio-economic circumstance are at a particular disadvantage. Furthermore differences in the accessibility of school systems and the quality of schools may result in the clustering of large numbers of children with a migrant background in underperforming schools. Providing these children with a better chance to succeed in education could reduce their maginalisation, exclusion and alienation.

2.2.1 The Gap in Achievement

In a recent study reported on attainment by ethnicity, it was highlighted that Chinese and Indian ethnic groups have the highest level 2 and level 3 attainment by age 19. Black, Traveller of Irish heritage, and Gypsy/Roma groups have the lowest attainment by age 19. It was also noted that the L2 attainment gap between the black and other ethnic groups closes to some extent between ages 16 and 19. When comparing the Asian group to the white and mixed ethnic groups, the L2 attainment gap increases between ages 16 and 17, then remains fairly constant. It was also noted that the black group shows the most improvement in L2 attainment for age 19 in 2006 cohort between ages 16 and 19, whereas the white group shows least improvement. The Asian group has the highest L2 attainment at age 16 and 19.

A detailed analysis of the study indicated that, for the age 19 in 2006 cohort, the top five highest-achieving ethnic groups in terms of L2 attainment were the following: Chinese (89.9 per cent), Indian (84.4 per cent), white and Asian (79.1 per cent), other Asian (78.9 per cent), and Irish (74.1 per cent). However, for those who were 19 in 2006 cohort, the five lowest-achieving detailed ethnic groups in terms of L2 attainment were the following: Caribbean (59.5 per cent), white and black Caribbean (59.1 per cent), other black (58.6 per cent), Traveller of Irish heritage (54.7 per cent), and Gypsy/Roma (38.6 per cent). Another study entitled 'Ethnic Minority Achievement Grant: Analysis of LEA Action Plans' conducted by Tikly et al, (2002), concluded after a series of data analysis that 'Bangladeshi, Pakistani, Black Caribbean pupils are achieving on average below the level of their groups. However, there is some evidence to show that Bangladeshi and Pakistani pupils are improving at a higher rate than average, leading to some narrowing of the attainment gap. The improvement rate for Black Caribbean pupils is on average, similar to or below that of other groups so the performance gap has not closed.

GILBERT GBEDAWO

Gillborn (2008), drew on the findings of the Youth Cohort Study (YCS) which indicated the changing patterns of GCSE attainment from the late 1980s to 2004. He stated that 'only one of the ethnic groups identified by the YCS has enjoyed improvement in every one of the surveys since 1989: White students. The performance of the other groups have been less certain, with periods where their attainment in one study remained static or actually fell below that of the previous survey.' Gillborn (2008), further noted that over the entire period, the proportion of black students attaining at least five higher grades almost doubled from 18 per cent to 34 per cent. This improvement (of 16 percentage points), however, did not keep pace with white students, whose attainment improved by 25 percentage points over the same period. Despite the improvements, therefore, it remains the case that the black–white gap is significantly larger (at 21 percentage points) than it was more than fifteen years ago (12 percentage points in 1989). Interestingly, Gillborn (2008), noted the following, 'the data shows that the black-white gap grew considerably during the early to mid 1990s. This was a period of intense emphasis on raising exam performance and improving positions in the newly introduced school performance tables first published for secondary schools in 1992. In contrast, surveys in 1998 and 2000 showed a narrowing of the black-white gap'.

However, it should be noted that since 1998, the data includes the results in other forms of assessment that are counted as equivalent to GCSEs, including General National Vocational Qualifications (GNVQs). Evidence shows that black students are disproportionately entered for these lower-status examinations, which do not carry the same weight in competition for jobs or places in academic studies in higher education (Gillborn 2008: 59). On the contrary, Gillborn (2008) noted that Indian students have improved more than their white peers. Although the proportion attaining five or more higher grades remained static between 2000 and 2002, overall Indian students have improved from 38 per cent in 1992 to 72 per cent, an increase of 34 percentage points. It is almost double the white improvement (of 18 percentage points) over the same periods. Although the YCS shows a comprehensive indication of the attainments of the various ethnic groups from

1999 to 2004, it fails to highlight those of migrant students from various countries in the West African subregion. Instead they were lumped together as black African—this can be misleading. The data, however, is indicative of the gap that still exists between black students and the other students. As mentioned earlier, there is a plethora of reasons according for the gap in the educational attainment at GCSE.

I hereby examine some of the often-cited reasons for this gap. Many scholars, in their efforts to explain the gap in attainment among various ethnic groups, have discovered that black students suffer the highest rate from exclusions from schools. Gilborn (2008), indicated that 'the most serious sanction that an English school can take against a student is to permanently expel them'. The reason he cited for the severity of exclusion is that 'young people excluded from school are much less likely to achieve 5 GCSEs at grade A*–C than other groups—just one in five young people compared to more than half overall'.

More than four times as many young people excluded from school fail to gain any qualifications at age 16 compared with those not excluded. Being out of school is a major risk factor for juvenile offending.

Research has found an almost direct correlation between youth crime rates in an area and the out-of-school population. Young people excluded from school are more than twice as likely to report having committed a crime as young people in mainstream school. Commenting further on the issue of exclusion, Gillborn (2008: 63) reiterated that 'when we focus on the likelihood of exclusion within each ethnic group some consistent patterns begin to emerge. Students of "South Asian" ethnic heritage, for example, have almost always been less likely to be excluded (as a percentage of their ethnic group) than their White and Black counterparts. In contrast Black Students (those categorised as Black Caribbean, Black African or Black other) have almost always been more likely to be excluded than their White peers: a pattern that is true in every year and for each of the Black groups.'

As rightly enunciated by Gillborn (2008), the over-exclusion of black students frequently emerges as one of the most important issues in the eyes of black teachers, parents, and students. It is also an area where public debate seems entirely immune to evidence. Despite academic research and community-based initiatives that highlight the inequitable treatment of black students in schools, the popular media continue to repeat crude stereotypes that reinforce powerful deficit images of black communities in general and black young men in particular. Nevertheless, there is compelling evidence that the over-representation of African Caribbean students in exclusions is the result of harsher treatment by schools rather than simple difference by students. A black scholar, Coard, (2007), however, identifies three main reasons why black children, especially of West Indian heritage, are failing to perform to the best of their abilities.

Coard (2007: 39) argued that 'there are three main ways in which a teacher can seriously affect the performance of a Black child: by being openly prejudiced; by being patronising; and by having low expectations of the child's abilities. All three attitudes can be found among teachers in this country. Indeed, these attitudes are widespread. The effect on the Black Child is enormous and devastating.' Coard (2007), further contested that 'most teachers absorb the brainwashing that everybody else in the society has absorbed—that Black people are inferior, are less intelligent etc., than white people. Therefore the Black child is expected to do less well in school.' On the premise of this argument, Coard (2007), concluded that 'the Black Child labours under three crucial handicaps: (1) Low expectations on his part about his likely performance in a white-controlled system of education; (2) Low motivation to succeed academically because he feels the cards are stacked against him; and finally, (3) Low teacher-expectations which affect the amount of effort expended on his behalf by the teacher, and also affect his own image of himself and his abilities.'

In contrast to the arguments put forward by Coard (2007) for black underachievement, Brown (2007: 75) cited how the government's race relation advisors put the blame on black underachievement on cultural differences, lack of understanding of English society and systems, and language problems. He noted that 'it was a policy based on no blame to either the host community or its institutions, and placed the "main blame" for underachievement at the door of the Black person'.

A counterargument put forward by Gillborn (2007) indicated that a consistent finding in both the US and UK is that, where education systems use some form of internal differentiation (through tracking, setting, boarding, streaming), black pupils are usually overrepresented in the lowest status groups. These groups typically receive poorer resources and are often taught by less-experienced (and/or less-successful) teachers. He further noted that these lower-ranked groups are not overtly determined on the basis of ethnic origin; they are usually presented as a reflection of the pupils' capabilities—that is, their abilities. It is, henceforth, not shocking when another black scholar, Mirza, reinforced the views of Gillborn when she wrote that 'if we look at the racialisation of education in Britain over the last 35 years we see patterns of persistent discrimination, both blatant and subtle. We can also map trends in our most subtle theories and approaches to Black educational underachievement. Both then and now we can see policy responses based on low or differential ability and intelligence, such as testing, setting and streaming' (Mirza 2007: 114).

Other writers cited institutional racism as the main cause for the underachievement of black minority ethnic communities (Byfield 2008). In addition to the above causes of low educational attainment among black students, Byfield (2008: 28), however, maintains that 'one should not overlook the wider structural issues associated with educational attainment. The insight students offered into the environments in which they lived their daily lives sheds some light on the complex social problems confronting them and the potentially adverse impact on them and their education. Most of them lived in poverty stricken communities where educational standards were low, resources were scarce and where they were surrounded by environmental, moral and social degradation.'

GILBERT GBEDAWO

Furthermore, Byfield noted that 'Black parents are often pathologies for the educational underachievement of their sons' (Byfield 2008: 29) but he concluded that 'many of the factors associated with the parents of Black boys who underachieve are also evident amongst some of the parents of those students'. Tomlinson's studies (Tomlinson 2008) support the findings from Byfield's study about the constraints of black parents' involvement in the education of their children, stating, 'Whilst some had the little choice about attending Parents' Evenings, others made an informed decision not to attend because they found them unproductive.' Apart from all the reasons for the gap in the attainment between black students and other ethnic groups, the OECD research findings based on factors that affect *immigrant* students highlighted the following:

1. There are marked performance differences in reading between native and immigrant students at age 15 in many, but not all, OECD countries.
2. Despite the observed performance gap in primary education, immigrant students perform around or above the international average in reading test (500 points) in primary education in all countries except France, Norway, Spain, and the United Kingdom.
3. The average performance disadvantage for immigrant students diminishes when taking into account that immigrant student are more likely to come from less socio-economically advantaged families, but it remains significant in many countries.
4. Immigrant students are less likely to participate in early childhood and care institutions which appear to facilitate the integration of immigrant students.
5. Immigrant students are more likely than native students to be enrolled in urban schools with high concentrations of students from immigrant and/or less-advantaged socio-economic backgrounds. They are more likely to enrol in lower-level and vocational programmes and less likely to enrol in academic programmes leading to advanced qualifications.

6. Immigrant students in some countries are more likely than native peers to attend schools with less-favourable learning environments according to the results from PISA 2003 (OECD 2006). In these countries, immigrants are more likely to be in a school environment characterised by high levels of student absenteeism and a poor disciplinary climate.

The above-stated facts in conjunction with already discussed ones paint a clear picture of challenges confronting migrant students in general and black students in particular. Strand (2008), on the other hand, noted that four factors have particularly large associations with attainment and progress. These are pupil's educational aspirations, parent's educational aspiration for their child, pupils' academic self-concept, and frequency of completing homework. He further noted that these factors play an important role in accounting for the greater progress during secondary school and the high attainment at age 16 of most minority ethnic groups, as well as the low-attaining white British pupils from low socio-economic classification (SEC) homes.

However, there are still questions about why, in particular, black Caribbean and black African boys from high SEC homes underachieve relative to their white British peers despite the high aspirations of the pupils and their parents' positive attitudes to school and high frequency of undertaking homework.

The government of the UK had made some interventions to close the gap in attainment and achievement among the different groups. Some of these inputs are policy-oriented while others target educational practices and financial support geared towards the purpose of reducing the attainment gap. The Excellence in Cities (EiC) policy was launched in 1999 with the aim of improving the attainment of all pupils in disadvantaged urban areas. Further phases were launched in 2000 and 2001 when EiC covered about a third of the secondary schools in England and when over 60 per cent of the minority ethnic pupils in England attended schools in EiC areas. Kendal et al. (2005), reported that 'Black pupils also had lower levels of attainment than pupils from White UK backgrounds at Key Stages 2 and 3. However, during Key

GILBERT GBEDAWO

Stage 4, pupils from Black African backgrounds made relatively good progress and by the end of the Key Stage their attainment was similar to that of White UK pupils in EiC Phase 1 areas and slightly below those of White UK pupils in non-EiC areas.'

The report also indicated that 'using the indicators based on GCSE point scores, in non-EiC areas pupils from all minority ethnic groups had higher levels of attainment than those from White UK backgrounds when school—and pupil—level factors (including attainment at end of Key Stage 3) were taken into account. Attending an EiC Phase 1 school was associated with improved attainment, relative to pupils from similar backgrounds in non-EiC areas for pupils from White non-UK, Black Caribbean, Black African, Bangladeshi and Chinese backgrounds (using points-based measures) pupils from Black Other and Other backgrounds and pupils from Indian backgrounds (capped point score) and girls from India backgrounds (uncapped scores) and pupils from Pakistani backgrounds (capped score only) but with a reduced probability of achieving at least five good GCSEs.'

Another major intervention was the allocation of the ethnic minority achievement grant (EMAG) to local educational authorities (LEAs) to help raise the achievement of minority ethnic pupils. A research led by Tikly (2002), into the impact of the EMAG funds and the analysis of LEA action plans revealed that 'in LEAs that have succeeded in raising the attainment of pupils of Black Caribbean heritage there is more support for providing supplementary schools as well as role models and mentors for pupils at risk of underachieving. Providing mentors and role models is also popular amongst LEAs that have been successful at improving Pakistani heritage pupils attaining at GCSE. Strategies aimed at involving parents and the Community were another common feature of the more successful LEAs including consultation with minority ethnic group over the use of EMAG, facilitating home/school visits, the establishment of support groups for specific groups of minority ethnic learners and parents' (DfES 2002).

In addition, another major attempt targeted at reducing the attainment gap between black African Caribbean pupils and other ethnic minorities was the Aiming High initiative. The Aiming High: African Caribbean Achievement Project, which was launched by the DfES in November 2003, aims to work with leaders of schools to develop a whole school approach to raise the achievement of African Caribbean pupils (DFES, 2003).

It was documented in a research led by Prof. David Gillborn (2006) that results for African Caribbean pupils attending Aiming High schools also improved at key stage 4. For example, the percentage of black Caribbean boys achieving five or more A*–C grades improved by 5.4 percentage points between 2003 and 2005, and for black Caribbean girls, it improved by 6.9 percentage points. However, these improvement rates were lower than the average for Aiming High schools (7 percentage points) and lower than the national average for black Caribbean pupils (8 percentage points), showing that gaps have not been closed.

It is clear from the interventions described above that, though some improvements have been made, the overall situation of underachievement of black students has not significantly improved. My question is, what can migrant parents do to close the achievement gap? Another question is, if supplementary schools seem to be making a positive contribution towards the successful education of these students, how and what are they doing differently? These questions are worth investigating as some useful lessons may be learned to help close the gap in the educational attainment of migrant students and the rest of the students' population in UK secondary schools.

2.3   Why Do Black Migrant Children Underachieve?

Although Gillborn (2007), noted that 'black children are intelligent, motivated and aspire to high achievement for themselves and their families', he blatantly also indicated that 'these attributes are not enough to guarantee success'. In a similar tone, Abbott (2007), also reiterated that 'when African and Afro-Caribbean children enter the school system at five they do as well as white and Asian children in tests. By 11 their achievement levels begin to drop off. By 16 there has been a collapse. And this is particularly true of Black boys—48 percent of all 16-year-old boys gain five GCSEs, grades A to E. Only 13 percent of Black boys in London achieve this standard. In some boroughs the figure is even worse.' This is further confirmed in a study by Gillborn and Mirza (Ofsted 2000), who reported that 'although Black pupils in general begin their school career ahead of all other groups of pupils, by the age of 15 they are significantly below all other groups'.

Livingstone (2007), argued that 'gaining good GCSEs is the first stage to securing employability and establishing a skills base for further training and higher education. Deprived of these qualifications, generations of Black youth are effectively consigned to low paid, unskilled jobs and years of unemployment. The effect of years of failure to educate Black children has been catastrophic for these young people and their families.'

The question is, what are the barriers to the educational excellence of black children in general and migrant children from Africa in particular? What can be done to address these impediments on the pathway to educational success of migrant children? Another key question is, what are the experiences of migrant children in the UK secondary schools?

Bernard Coard's groundbreaking seminal study 'The Scandal of the Black Child in Schools in Britain' in 1971 documented and revealed some of the challenges regarding the academic progress and success of black children. Ouseley (2007), recounted that 'Bernard Coard's work has withstood the test of time because the problems facing African-Caribbean parents and their children have fundamentally remained the same. Racism, race prejudice and social inequalities are crucial factors in the perpetuation of educational policies and practices which cause the system to fail the African-Caribbean communities. These will prevail even though there have been some changes and new developments in the intervening 20 year period.'

Ken Livingstone (2007), noted that 'African pupils are generally achieving more highly than African-Caribbean pupils, this is often only marginal'. This observation on the part of Livingstone suggests that the African migrant children like the African Caribbean children in the UK secondary schools are predisposed to similar challenges of educational disadvantage.

It is my view that some of the educational disadvantage may have its roots in the lack of understanding of the cultural and socio-economic challenges that often plague ethnic minorities and migrants. There is hope for the future when we understand the challenge and develop strategies to right the wrong.

Gillborn (2007), however, conceded, saying, 'And yet we still endure a system that fails a disproportionate numbers of Black children, excludes many from mainstream schooling altogether, and channels others into second class courses deemed more appropriate by a teaching force that continues to be unrepresentative of the community it serves.' Gillborn, like Coard 39 years ago, argued that there is a need for radical change and reform. Gillborn (2007), therefore, proposed that 'for real change to happen, race equality must be mainstream and mandatory for all schools'. There is a plethora of reasons cited in academic literature to explain the rationale behind the underachievement of migrant children. Among such are the following: lack of black teachers who should act as role models to inspire and motivate the black children (McFarlane 2007; Hall 2007); lack of internal cohesion, leadership, and clout among black communities (Muir 2007; Leary 2005); high rate of exclusion from mainstream education (Mahamdallie 2007). Cole and Blair (2006) noted that 'Black pupils/students in particular were over-represented in suspensions and expulsions from school, and in units for pupils/ students with emotional and behavioural difficulties, and were clearly not performing to the same level as their white peers in public examination'. Other reasons cited for underachievement include the following: a decline in parental involvement, an increase in peer pressure, a decline in nurturance and an increase in discipline problems, a decline in teacher expectations, a lack of understanding of learning style, and a lack of male teachers (Kunjufu 1990).

Another powerful argument put forward by Joy Leary for black children's failure lies in what she called the post-traumatic slave syndrome. She contested that slavery has handed to black children debilitating effects which predispose them to mindsets, attitudes, habits, and belief systems which result eventually in failure and impotence. She wrote that 'today the legacy of slavery and oppression remains etched in our souls. The impacts of our history can be witnessed daily in our struggle to understand who and what we are, and in our jaundiced vision of who and what we can become. The impacts of our history can be witnessed in our continual fight for respect, respect that we seek and demand from without, but that can only be built from within. These impacts can be witnessed in the war between affirmative racial socialization in our homes and destructive racist socialization everywhere else, a war that I'm sorry to say, we seem to be losing' (Leary 2005).

How then do we reverse the tide and win the war? What should we do to make sure those migrant children in UK secondary schools attain educational excellence? Supplementary schools, through active parental involvement, have been highlighted as the means towards educational excellence of migrant children.

2.4 The Role and Contributions of Supplementary Schools

Community schools, often known as supplementary or complementary schools, have been an important component of the educational experience of many ethnic minority children in Britain. These schools are socio-educational institutions established and run by ethnic minority communities and have a diverse and distinctive pedagogy and aims influenced by the community's needs within specific political and social cultural contexts (Prokopiou and Cline 2010). 'Community schools not only reflect the linguistic and cultural diversity in mainstream society but a powerful reminder of Britain's failure to meet the needs of children of different communities who attend them' (Pantazi 2010). About

STEPS TOWARDS EDUCATIONAL EXCELLENCE

four decades ago, Coard (1971), recommended the establishment of black supplementary schools throughout Britain with the view of addressing 'the inadequacies of the British school system, and for its refusal to teach our children our history and culture'. In response to the inequalities, discrimination, prejudice, and racism facing migrant students in schools, black parents started supplementary schools or Saturday schools to remedy the situation.

'Supplementary schools were intended to counteract some of the distortions of history, the misinformation and the inadequate academic instruction which parents believed their children were receiving' (Chevannes and Reeves 2006). 'The complementary schools were set up for more than just the maintenance of cultural, linguistic values and ethnic identity' (Taylor 2009). Several black complementary schools were a direct response to government policies and so-called compensatory initiatives to tackle black underachievement (Plowden Report DES 2009). Jones (1986:4), surmises that 'the school was formed to help bridge the gap between the educational needs of the Black children and the expectations of teachers in the State Schools! We hold the view that the underachievement is not the fault of our children nor their parents. We set up supplementary schools because we have lost trust in the mainstream schools. Supplementary school provision, as far as we are concerned, is not strictly to provide for "underachievement". We believe we should continue the tradition of providing, "classes", "lessons", "tuitions", to people of every level of educational ability.' Jones (1986: 4) also contends that 'Black children need motivation more than any other group in this community. The legacy of slavery and colonialism coupled with the prevailing policy of institutional racism make the emotional support more imperative.' It was these sentiments that galvanised the black community to start supplementary schools to motivate, enthuse, and provide a conducive and enabling environment where the educational, emotional, and holistic development of black children matters. In general, the contributions of supplementary schools to the educational attainment of migrant children who participate in them is a positive one (Issa and William 2009:19; www.multiverse.ac.uk).

GILBERT GBEDAWO

The government's decision to fund the National Resource Centre for supplementary schools in London is an indication that these schools are making a positive impact to the journey towards educational excellence of migrant children in our UK secondary schools. According to the DCSF (2010: 27), 'In general supplementary schools offer a wide range of out-of-school hours educational provision for children and young people of shared ethnic, cultural or linguistic heritage, provided by volunteers in the community however the report noted that the National Resource Centre (NRC) defines supplementary schools as: Supplementary schools (sometimes known as Complementary Schools, Saturday Schools or Mother-tongue Schools) normally operate outside of normal school hours typically at the weekend, evenings or in the school holidays.'

Supplementary schools are community-inspired education initiatives. Normally, these have been set up by communities in response to a perceived need by parents or the community. This can include support for mainstream learning but could also include home-language teaching, cultural instruction, and religious instruction. Some supplementary schools may also run other activities, such as family-based learning, sports activities, or other activities helpful to the community, such as advice on avoiding anti-social behaviour, and sexual health (NRC website). The DCSF research report noted that 'the term "supplementary school" was initially coined to illustrate that these schools were organised for and by minority ethnic communities and provided education, or as a supplement to mainstream schooling' (Richards et al. 2010).

The report shows that 'supplementary schools grew significantly in the second half of the twentieth century after Wold War 2 with the arrival of refugees from Eastern Europe and during later periods of immigration from Commonwealth countries and the number of supplementary schools increased again more recently with the arrival of refugees and asylum seeking communities from war- torn countries' (Tomlinson et al. 2010). Generally, there are two reasons for the existence of supplementary schools in the UK—firstly, the supplementary schools were set up by minority ethnic community members to preserve their cultural/ethnic identities and/or faith/traditions (Creese et al. 2010) and, secondly, supplementary schools were established to cater for what minority ethnic parents considered to be lacking in the mainstream education system (Hall et al. 2010). Another important aspect of supplementary schools is how they have been categorised based on their overriding principles and ethos.

Issa and Williams (2009) have provided three categories of supplementary schools. The first category is designed to support children in mainstream educational subjects where the provision is intended to raise the level of success in educational attainment. This category is found especially amongst African Caribbean communities, where pupils have consistently had relatively lower levels of attainment.

The second category is made up of schools which aim to maintain the cultural and/or language traditions of a particular community. The final category of schools is organised to promote educational values and other values that are distinctly counter to the values found in mainstream education (DSCF 2010). However, one must be careful about these categorisations because the activities and the general operations of supplementary schools are constantly evolving due to the changing demands of parents, communities, but more importantly, government policies. Issa and Williams (2009: 12) indicated that 'government support Community for complementary provision began in the 1970s after the European Economic Community (EEC) declaration supporting the maintenance of the mother tongue of migrant children for the case of eventual return to the country of origin'.

There was initial resistance from the British government on grounds that the situation of the minorities did not constitute 'migrant status'. Eventually, pressure from Europe and community groups in the UK forced the government to back down. Over the years, the government has increasingly recognised the contribution that supplementary schools can make towards the education of young people; therefore, from 2001–2004, the government funded the supplementary schools support services. Further recognition came with the publication of *Aiming High: Raising Attainment for Minority Ethnic Pupils,* which was one of the first documents to refer to the role that supplementary schools play in many minority ethnic pupils lives and noted that 'many pupils have also benefited greatly from out-of-hours learning in community run initiatives such as supplementary schools' (DFES 2003). The government's first serious step towards supporting the complementary schools' sector came with its fairly recent decision to fund the National Resource Centre (NRC) for supplementary schools in London. This had been running as the only resource centre for supplementary and mother tongue schools in England for ten years before merging with ContinYou in 2006 (Issa and Williams 2009: 15).

The NRC aims to work with supplementary school leaders, education professional, and campaigners to:

- raise standards in supplementary education
- raise the profile of supplementary schools and what they can achieve
- raise funds for supplementary schools.

The above three areas also reflect governmental concerns about the quality of education in supplementary schools and the type of teaching resources they have access to. The fact is that supplementary school funding is insecure, and that some suffer from high turnover of staff (ContinYou 2010). The NRC has also set up a code of practice and the quality framework for supplementary schools to enhance the work they do, but Sedon et al. argued that these could 'stifle the freedom and greatest assets of the sector' (Sedon et al. 2010).

2.5   Supplementary Schools and Attainment

In the recent study conducted by the DCSF into the impact of supplementary schools on pupils' attainment, it was admitted that 'limited research exists about supplementary schools and except for Strands (2007) research, the published studies are small-scale and unevenly distributed across Jewish, Chinese, Asian, Turkish and

Black groups, there is immense variety amongst supplementary schools, therefore they should not be viewed as representing one community or type of provision, it is not clear the extent to which pupils attendance at supplementary schools varies and that the benefits of supplementary schools to mainstream education will vary with the purpose of the school' (DCSF 2010).

In spite of the above findings, Issa and Williams (2009: 131) wrote that 'complementary schools can engender positive aspirations in Black children and counter the stereotype of the underachievement'. This assertion is consistent with Reay and Mirza, who argued that 'the organisation of these institutions was based on both need and mutual respect. The teachers and students shared a common ethnic background and the antagonism between Black boys (students) and White teachers were absent. The supplementary schools were in addition to regular schools but they attempted to reinforce the mainstream curriculum. They usually did this by having a Black teaching force, engaged in references to Black culture and enforced the idea that Black people had to work twice as hard as others to be academically successful' (Reay and Mirza 2009).

As proposed by Barber (2001), 'many schools improve inspiration and motivation to learn are more likely to come from children who benefit from involvement in out of school activities as well as formal schooling'. Policymakers, he suggested, would have to think beyond the school, to the elements of learning which had been previously left to chance. One of those areas was learning at home, and another was organised learning out of school because the benefits children reap are incalculable. These activities are educationally wonderful.

They provide a wide range of activities in which young people can discover their talents and find success. They provide opportunities for praise, the key to so much progress. They broaden horizons and execute imaginations, and since they are largely voluntary, they provide regular benefits of choosing to learn and to achieve. All this is in addition to whatever discipline or set of skills are being taught. These kinds of opportunities are, therefore, extremely important to young peoples' all-around competence and profile of intelligences and to their self-esteem.

They can be vital in developing among young people the motivation to learn and to continue learning for their own sake (Barber 2001). Supplementary schools have a huge potential and have demonstrated that they contribute to the educational attainment of minority ethnic students, which is evident in 'the experiences of complementary school students which are generally found to be positive' (Issa and Williams 2009: 19). However, the fact remains that, owing to the limited research on supplementary schools, it is not conclusive to what extent supplementary schools are contributing to the educational excellence of students. However, as noted by Halpern (2005: 148), research has found that social capital plays a similar general role in the educational achievements of ethnic groups and of the white majority as the evidence is now beyond dispute. When schools work together with families to support learning, children tend to succeed not just in school but throughout life. When parents are involved in their children's education at home, their children do better in school. When parents are involved at school, their children go further in school, and the school they go to are better (Henderson and Berla 2005).

2.6 Conclusion

In conclusion, the literature demonstrates the reasons for the existence of supplementary schools, the perceived benefits of the sector, and the government's interest to improve and regulate its provision, but equally, it admits the limited research done so far on its potential to contribute to the educational attainment of minority ethnic students, although there is an admission that supplementary schools are making a positive difference. I would, therefore, contribute to the evolving area of knowledge on supplementary school through this book. Hence, my aim is to find out, how supplementary schools are contributing to the educational attainment of migrants from across the world especially Africa.

CHAPTER 3

Methods and Methodology

3.1 Introduction

This chapter focuses on the research methodology used for this study. An outline of the human capital theory and social capital theory are stated first. The research context, which is a supplementary school focusing on the provision of Saturday school for migrant children especially from Africa, is then given to allow readers to be familiar with the context where the study was carried. The research tools used to collect data are interviews and data analysis. The procedure for data analysis, validity of the research findings, limitations of the study, and research ethics are outlined and discussed as well.

3.2 Human Capital Theory (HCT)

'Broadly human capital refers to knowledge, skills and qualifications' (Schuller et al. 2005: 5). Schuller et al. shows the meaning of human capital succinctly when they wrote: 'McCloskey describes the revelation of the idea of human capital for Schulz who interviewed an old and poor farm couple and was struck by how content they seemed. "Why are you so content," he asked, "though very poor?" They answer: "You are wrong Professor. We are not poor, we've used up our farm to educate four

GILBERT GBEDAWO

children through college, remaking fertile land and well-stocked pens into knowledge of Law and Latin. We are rich."'

'This is a definition based on the idea that, rather than investing assets in physical capital or consuming them, education is an investment in the stock of skills to earn a future return. Hence the metaphor implicit in the term "human capital" relates to investment and to the notion of using resources to build up a stock of additional resources (human capital) that will earn a return' (Schuller et al. 2005: 7).

The basic underlying argument of the HCT is that investment in education leads to greater productivity and, subsequently, to greater earnings. In a joint paper by Swedish ministry of finance, German ministry of finance, and HM Treasury in 2008, it was noted that 'in today's integrated global economy Europe is often competing by producing high-tech, high value added goods and services. This shift towards a more knowledge based economy is placing greater emphasis on the skills of the workforce. As new jobs demand new and often more advanced skills, each generation entering the labour market needs to be better educated and better trained than the previous generation. At the same time rapid technological and structural change means that people also need to retain and update their skills throughout their working lives' (HM Treasury 2008).

The underlying basis for the above assertion is that 'economic research shows human capital to be a key determinant of productivity, wages and economic growth: At the micro-economic level: there is clear evidence that school attainment is a primary determinant of an individual's future income and labour prospects. An additional year of schooling increases wages at the individual level on average by around 7 percent across European countries; lifetime earnings for graduates are almost 60 percent higher than those with only an upper secondary education, and firm-level data show that a highly skilled workforce increases a company's productivity innovation and long term competitions. At the macro-economic level: evidence shows human capital is an important determinant of productivity and growth, although uncertainty remains about the size of its effect; and a recent study by the Lisbon Council and the OECD estimates that an additional year of education could increase productivity and economic output by between 3 and 6 percent' (OECD Education 2008)

3.3 Social Capital Theory

Baron et al. (2000: 1) defines social capital broadly as 'social networks, the reciprocities that arise from them and the value of these for achieving mutual goals'. Social capital derived its prominence from the seminal work of Bourdieu, Coleman, and Putnam, so let us capture the views of these scholars that brought the term to the political, social, economic, and intellectual limelight and stage. Bourdieu's definition of 'social capital' is 'the aggregate of the actual or potential resources which are linked to possession of desirable network of more or less institutionalised relationships of mutual acquaintance and recognition which provides each of its members with the backing of collectively-owned capital' (Bourdieu 2000: 5). However, Fine (2001: 53–64) argues about the failure of Bourdieu to capture and articulate intellectually and contextually the meaning of social capital due to the multifarious use of the term 'capital'. Fine documented this when he wrote, 'For whilst Bourdieu's approach to social capital is itself fundamentally flawed and might in some respects be judged to have supported the path taken by the vast majority of the literature that abandoned him, his own theory has sufficient critical content to have scuttled what social capital has become.'

Fine went on further to highlight three particular features of Bourdieu's work on social capital: 'First he [referring to Bourdieu] pursues highly fluid notion of capital, second it remains highly socially and historically contextual and third, his work—not least in light of the previous aspect—has been discarded as social capital literature has evolved.'

The second major proponent of social capital was Coleman. For Coleman, social capital was significant primarily as a way of understanding the relationship between educational achievement and social inequality (Baron et al. 2000: 5). They noted the succinct and somehow explicit definition of 'social capital' by Coleman as 'the set of resources that are inherent in family relations and in community social organisation and that are useful for the cognitive or social development of a child or young person' (Coleman 2000). Social relations, Coleman argued, constituted useful capital resources for actors through the process of establishing obligations, expectations, and trustworthiness, creating channels for information, and setting norms backed by efficient sanctions (Coleman 2000).

The difference between Coleman's and Bourdieu's depictions of social capital to denote the ways in which elite groups use their contacts to reproduce their privilege is that Coleman extended the scope of the concept to encompass the social relationships of non-elite groups (Baron et al. 2000: 8). Finally, let us consider Robert Putnam's view of social capital, bearing in mind that it was Putnam who has made the term very popular. According to him, 'Social capital means the features of social life, networks, norms, and trust that enable participants to act together more effectively to pursue shared objectives' (Putnam 2000). Putnam went further to make a distinction between bonding social capital and bridging social capital. Bonding social capital refers to the links between like-minded people, or the reinforcement of homogeneity. This builds strong ties but can also result in higher walls, excluding those who do not qualify. On the other hand, bridging social capital refers to the building of connections between heterogeneous groups, which are likely to be more fragile but more likely also to foster social inclusion (Baron et al. 2000: 10).

'A mainstream view of the relation between education and social inequality is that social class advantage breeds educational advantage. According to this view, poor performance and low attainment are mainly due to socially structured disadvantage. Some groups are favoured because the social circumstances of their upbringing and the resources which their families possess make it easier to stay in the system in order to reap its rewards' (Lauglo 2000: 142).

The above quote presupposes that social capital of the migrant students is a crucial determinant of the educational outcomes of students. Research has shown that the human and financial capital of the parents help to predict the educational success or failure of children. But significant amount of the remaining variance is explained by social capital, and social capital also helps to explain the impact of the parents' human and financial resources (Halpern 2005: 143).

Bourdieu's particular claim is that in order to succeed, especially in the selective stages of the system, you also need to be at ease with the lifestyle which is taken for granted among those who have high status in this social field: the nuances of language, the aesthetic preferences, and other symbolic expressions which mark the insider against the outsider. Such elements are not just accoutrements of cultural privilege, according to Bourdieu; they serve as prerequisites for success. It would seem that the further one's origin is from a country's cultural elite, the fewer are one's chances of doing well in school. By this line of reasoning, migrant children are destined to fail in school (Lauglo 2000: 14). It is therefore imperative to turn to black supplementary schools to find ways in which they provide migrant students with the much-needed social capital to ameliorate educational disadvantage and set them on the pathway to educational excellence.

3.4 Research Context

The research was conducted in a supplementary school based in the Borough of Southwark, south-eastern part of London. The choice of this school was due to the following reasons:

1. It provides support to predominantly migrant students from Africa.
2. It is situated in a borough with over fifty per cent of minority ethnic groups in secondary schools.
3. The time for the study is limited, coupled with the fact that I have a previous working relationship with the school as the coordinator of the secondary phase of the school.

GILBERT GBEDAWO

3.5 Research Design and Strategy

Case study research excels at bringing us to an understanding of a complex issue or objects and can extend experience or add strength to what is already known through previous research. Case studies emphasise detailed contextual analysis of a limited number of events or conditions and their relationships. Social scientists, in particular, have made wide use of this qualitative research method to examine contemporary real-life situations and provide the basis for the application of ideas and extension of methods (Soy 1997). However, the following criticisms have been made against case study method:

1. The study of a small number of cases can offer no grounds for establishing reliability or generality of findings.
2. Others feel that the intense exposure to study of the case biases the findings.
3. Some dismiss case study research as useful only as exploratory tool.

However, as noted by Yin (2009: 2), 'Case studies are the preferred method when a) "how" or "why" questions are being posed b) the investigator has little control over events, and c) the focus is on a contemporary phenomenon within a real-life context'. Yin (2009: 11) also argued that 'case study is preferred in examining contemporary events, but when the relevant behaviour cannot be manipulated. The case study relies on many of the same techniques as history but it adds two sources of evidence not usually included in the historian's repertoire, direct observation of the events being studied and interviews of the persons involved in the events . . . the case study's unique strength is its ability to deal with a full variety of evidence—documents, artefacts, interviews and observations—beyond what might be available in a conventional historical study. Moreover, in some situations, such as participant-observation, informal manipulation can occur.'

My study sets out to answer the following questions:

1. What are the experiences of migrant children in supplementary schools in relation to mainstream schools?
2. How are supplementary schools contributing to the educational attainment of migrant children from Africa?
3. How are parents involved in supplementary schools?

Due to lack of research into the experiences of migrant children and how supplementary schools contribute to the educational attainment of these students, I employed a case study as it gives depth in the data and explores extensively the underlying issues. I also used purposeful sampling technique and included a range of migrant students from across Africa, although the findings may be applicable to the experiences of migrant children in general and most of the parents.

I have chosen the director and the management of the organisation as part of those interviewed because I wanted to elicit from them the rationale for starting up this particular supplementary school, the contributions and impacts they have made on migrant students, and the future and direction of the organisation. I have chosen to interview the students to capture first-hand their own experiences in mainstream educational institutions and why they have chosen to attend the supplementary school. I also wanted to know their views in terms of the supplementary school. I also chose to interview parents to find out why they have enrolled their children in the supplementary schools and to document their views on how the supplementary school affects the educational experiences of their children. Finally, teachers were also chosen to find out the type of educational intervention they were providing and how that differs from the mainstream provision.

3.6 Interviewing

Yin (2009: 106) noted that 'one of the most important sources of case study information is the interview however; interviews also are essential sources of case study information. The interviews will be guided conversation rather than structured queries.' According to Rubin and Rubin, 'The interviews will be guided conversations rather than structured queries. In order words, although you will be pursuing a consistent line of enquiry, your actual stream of questions in a case study interview is likely to be fluid rather than rigid' (Rubin and Rubin 2009). Yin (2009: 107) made a clear distinction between the three types of interviews:

1. In an in-depth interview, you may ask key respondents about the facts of a matter as well as their opinions about events. In some situations, you may even ask the interviewee to propose his or her own insights into certain occurrences and may use such propositions as the basis for further inquiry.
2. Focused interview takes place over a short period of an hour. In such cases, the interview may still remain open-ended and assume a conversational manner, but you are more likely to be following a certain set of questions derived from the case study protocol.
3. The third type of interview entails more structured questions along the lines of formal survey. Such a survey could be designed as part of an embedded case study and produce quantitative data as part of the case study evidence.

3.7   Disadvantages of Interviewing

Byfield (2008: 7) wrote that like any method of data collection, qualitative interviewing is not free of problems. There are artefacts intrinsic to qualitative research methods, including interviews that affect the reliability of the data produced. Like any self-report method, the interview approach relies upon respondents being able and willing to give accurate and complete answers to the questions. There is always the danger that interviewees might lie. They might wish to sabotage the research, dislike the interviewer, be too embarrassed to tell the truth, or simply not remember the details accurately.

Another limitation is that data generated can be difficult to analyse and compare. And like any method where the researcher is an overt participant in the data collection process, interviewing involves researcher effects.

Byfield also noted that 'in an interview, the characteristics of the researcher—for example: demeanour, accent, dress, gender, age or race- may influence the respondents' willingness to answer accurately'. Due to my personal background and common ethnicity with the interviewees, I was able to overcome some of the related challenges to interviewing as recounted by Robson when he wrote, 'But since people engage in more self-disclosure to an interviewer they find similar to themselves, the fact that that we share common ethnicity and nationality was an added advantage' (Robson 2008). I employed both closed- and open-ended questions in my interview framework to find answers to my research questions. Yin (2009: 114), however, proposed that multiple sources of evidence be used in case studies for the development of converging lines of enquiry. He argued that 'the use of multiple sources of evidence in case studies allows an investigator to address a broader range of historical and behavioural issues. Thus any case study finding or conclusion is likely to be more convincing and accurate if it is based on several different sources of information, following a corroboratory mode.'

3.8 Complexities of Methodology

Among other things, the main ethical issues confronted during the course of my research interview include confidentiality on the part of the interviewees and respondents. At first, they were apprehensive and anxious about sharing their views, their experiences, and the overall circumstances confronting and shaping their lives. They wanted to be assured of anonymity and that whatever has been shared with me would in no case incriminate them. I therefore ensured that those interviewed gave their informed consent, and to maintain the anonymity of the students, teachers, and the management, I used pseudonyms. The issues that were considered very sensitive and which evoked a lot of emotional feelings and sentiments were treated with the sensitivity and care they deserve. Such issues include migration, racial prejudice and discrimination, racism, and the lingering impacts and legacy of the trans-Atlantic slave trade.

Another significant ethical issue that surfaced during the research was my personal connection with the supplementary school as a teacher and the coordinator of teaching in the secondary phase. But more importantly, my perceived closeness and fondness with the founding members of the organisation and the director due to our common ethnic origin is a perceived asset. This is consistent with Yin (2009: 112) when commenting on participant observation: 'The most distinctive opportunity is related to your ability to gain access to events or groups that are otherwise inaccessible to study.' Other advantages he noted include the following: 'You have the ability to manipulate minor events—such as covering a meeting of a group of persons in the case.'

My connection, however, to the organisation has both advantages and disadvantages. The former includes but is not limited to openness and trust on the part of the interviewees as they were confident that nothing disclosed to me would be used against them. Another good side to this connectedness was that I was granted unreserved access to archival records and artefacts, which illuminated my research interests and data collection process. I must admit that I strongly support extra learning opportunities for young people, especially migrant communities, because of its potential benefits to those who participate in it and to the mainstream education. As a teacher in both mainstream education and the supplementary sector, I am mindful of the bias this might generate as noted by Bell (2005: 166) when she wrote that 'many factors can result in bias and there are always dangers in research carried out by individual researchers, particularly those who have strong view about the topic they are researching'.

Gray, in her doctoral study of truancy in Western Australian schools, was very conscious of the fact that she was researching a topic in which she had a keen interest and about which she held strong views. She recalled that it was her constant questioning of the practice and her critical attitude towards the interpretation of data which helped her to recognise signs of bias (Gray 2005). I therefore applied the same kind of discipline of constant critical questioning of data in the hope that it would prevent the occurrence of bias or minimise its effects.

My sole intention for undertaking this research is to understand the experiences of migrant children and understand the ways supplementary education provide them with the added stimuli on their pathway towards educational excellence. I attempted to represent the findings as accurately as possible, taking into account the evidence and questioning carefully the available data collected through interviews and data analysis of archival records and artefacts.

3.9 Document Analysis

Bell (2005: 122) is of the view that 'in some projects documentary analysis will be used to supplement information obtained by other methods, as for instance when the reliability of evidence gathered from interview of questionnaires is checked. In others, it will be essential or even exclusive method of research.' Bell further noticed that during the document search, it is helpful to clarify exactly what kind of documents exists. A 'document' is a general term for an impression left on a physical object by a human being. Research can involve analysis of photographs, films, videos. Slides and other non-written sources—all of which can be classed as documents (Bell 2005: 125). Yin promised that except for studies of preliterate societies, documentary information is likely to be relevant to every case study. This type of information can take many forms and should be the object of explicit data collection plans (Yin 2009: 101). Yin (2009: 103) then listed the following variety of documents:

1. letters, memoranda, email, correspondence, and other personal documents, such as diaries, calendars, and notes
2. agendas, announcements, minutes of meetings, and other written report of events

GILBERT GBEDAWO

3. administrative documents—proposals, progress reports, and other internal records
4. formal studies of evaluations of the same case that you are studying
5. news clippings and other articles appearing in the mass media or community newspapers.

For case studies, the most important use of documents is to corroborate and align evidence from other sources (Yin 2009: 103). Yin therefore listed three uses of documents. First, documents are helpful in verifying the correct spellings and titles or names of organisations that might have been mentioned in an interview. Second, documents can provide other specific details to corroborate information from other sources. Third, you can make inferences from documents (Yin 2009: 103). However, documents should be treated with caution because, as Yin warned, 'the casual investigator may mistakenly assume that all kinds of documents—including proposals for projects or programs—contain the unmitigated truth (Yin 2009: 105).

Table 1 Research Questions, Method, Expected Outcomes, and Data Source

Research Questions	Methods	Expected Outcome
1. What are the experiences of migrant children in UK secondary schools?	• interviews • documents analysis	mixed experiences (some positive and some negative)
2. How are supplementary schools contributing to the educational attainment of migrant children from Africa?	• document analysis • interviews	provision of small group learning, personalised learning, support homework, and black history celebration
3. Are migrant students from Africa achieving educational excellence in UK secondary schools?	• document analysis • interviews	There are gaps in key stages 1 and 2 but closes at key stages 3 and 4

Data Sources

Documents:

- annual reports
- minutes of meetings
- newsletters and publications
- video clips
- letters/correspondences
- questionnaires and feedbacks

Interviews:

- school director
- school founding member/secretary
- a group of six students
- five parents
- out-of-school-hours coordinator/LA officer
- five teachers

3.10 Interpreting the Data

The recorded interviews were transcribed soon after the interviewees completed the interview session to ensure that the views of the participants were accurately transcribed, documented, filed, and coded.

However, in some cases where the process was delayed for a day or two, it took careful listening over and over again due to variations in voice tones and quality. The overall process was smooth as I downloaded the voice recordings to a laptop and was able to increase the volume of the recorded interviews to enhance the transcription.

I must admit, however, that it took longer than anticipated to transcribe the voice recording, especially interviews that lasted beyond an hour and a half. This was rather daunting, considering the limitation of time. After reading the transcribed data, themes and patterns began to emerge. These themes and patterns helped me to categorise the findings based on the three types of research questions, which are:

1. experiences of migrant children in supplementary schools in relation to mainstream schools
2. the contributions of supplementary schools towards the educational attainment of migrant children
3. how parents are involved in supplementary schools.

In the same way, all documents were similarly treated for emerging themes and patterns. This is consistent with Bell (2005: 203), who wrote that 'raw data taken from questionnaires, interview schedules, check lists etc. need to be recorded, analysed and interpreted. A hundred separated pieces of interesting information will mean nothing to a researcher or a reader unless they have been categorised and interpreted. We are constantly looking for similarities and differences, for groupings, patterns and items of particular significance.'

3.11 Validation of Findings

As noted by Yin (2009: 40), 'Because a research design is supposed to represent a logical set of statements, you also can judge the quality of any given design according to certain logical tests. Concepts that have been offered for these tests include trustworthiness, credibility, conformability, and data dependability' (UK Government Accountability Office 2009). Kidder and Judd observed that there are four tests common to all social science methods, namely:

1. Construct validity: identifying correct operational measures for the concepts being studied.
2. Internal validity (for explanatory or casual studies only and not for descriptive or exploratory studies): seeking to establish a casual relationship, whereby certain conditions are believed to lead to other conditions as distinguished from spurious relationships.

3. External validity: defining the domain to which a study's findings can be generalised.
4. Reliability: demonstrating that the operations of a study—such as the data collection procedures—can be repeated with the same results.

In order to facilitate validation, I triangulated the data collected using different sources, such as interview, document analysis and observation.

3.12 Limitation of the Study

The study was intended to find out about the experiences of migrant students who are in secondary schools across the United Kingdom and also to explore the contributions of supplementary schools towards the educational attainment of these students, with the view of finding out if migrant students are achieving educational excellence in secondary schools in UK, using one supplementary school as a case study. It is therefore important to note that the findings of this study may not be applicable to other migrant students and supplementary schools due to differences in the experiences of other migrant communities, and the peculiarities of their socio-economic and cultural heritage by different supplementary schools may vary. However, these findings can serve as guidelines or starting points for discovering the potential of supplementary schools to unlocking the educational attainment of migrant students.

3.13 Ethical Consideration

The importance of ethical issues as far as the field of educational research is concerned cannot be underestimated. Hence, it is imperative that care and steps be taken to ensure that the expectations and the concerns of participants are thoroughly addressed. The following conditions and guarantees were presented to ensure that those needs are considered and addressed:

1. All participants were offered opportunity to remain anonymous.
2. All information was treated with the strictest confidentiality.
3. Interviewees had the opportunity to verify statements when the research was in draft form.
4. Participants will receive a copy of the final report (if they so wish).
5. The research attempted to explore educational management in practice.

It is hoped that the final report may be of benefit to the school and to those who took part (Bell 2005: 51–52).

In order to be consistent with Bell's approach above, I ensured that the whole aim of the research was discussed with the director of the organisation before the start of the data collection process. This enabled the leadership to give consent and support regarding data collection. A consent form and a letter of introduction were sent to the participants, and a consent form was signed and returned before the interview process.

The consent form guaranteed anonymity and confidentiality and explained the steps that would be followed to do so. The potential participants were also informed about their ability to withdraw from the process at any time if they so wish and their freedom to choose not to answer a particular question if they so wished.

I proceeded with the interview and recording after the participants gave their consent and the participants were not coerced to give any information. Contrary to the initial allocated time frame to collect data, I realised during the process that it would take longer due to unforeseen circumstances and unanticipated delays to get all participants interviewed. However, I managed to get an extension to collect the much-needed data.

The lesson learned from this is always to anticipate these situations as one is dealing with human beings whose schedule and circumstances can change at any point in time and so affect the researcher's ability to either gain access or carry out interviews.

3.14 Conclusion

This chapter shows the research context, which is a supplementary school based in the south-east of London, providing educational support and other services to migrant communities, especially those from Africa. The research has also identified the participants to be interviewed in order to answer the research questions. The researcher also thought that a case study is the best approach to understand how supplementary schools are contributing to the educational attainment of migrant students and, therefore, used qualitative research methods, such as document analysis and interviewing, as a means of data collection.

Other issues highlighted include validity and limitation of findings, ethical issues, and steps taken to assure participants of anonymity and confidentiality.

Participants Interviewed

Students	Teachers	Parents/Leadership
Adwoa	Amposah	Agbeke (director)
Yaw	Nana	Nat (LA officer)
Akosua	Edem	Aku (secretary)
Kodzo	Dodzi	Ansantewaa
Mensah	Korku	Maame
Korbla		Tevi
		Tega

CHAPTER 4

Finding of the Study

4.1 Introduction

The study is organised and presented in the light of the theoretical framework—human capital theory and social capital theory—as outlined in the previous chapters. The views of the students pertaining to their experiences in mainstream secondary schools and the supplementary schools have been documented. The chapter also explores how supplementary schools are positioned to contribute towards educational attainment of migrant children in the mainstream schools and the role of parents in unlocking the potential of their children as effective learners on the journey towards educational excellence. Furthermore, it examines the various activities carried out by supplementary school in its attempt to close the attainment gap between migrant students in the UK secondary schools and their counterparts.

Finally, it addresses the limitations and challenges of the supplementary schools and the implications on project delivery and sustenance.

4.2 Application of the HCT to the Supplementary School

The interviews of students, parents, teachers, and leadership of the YLN indicate a basic belief in human capital formation and development by various actors in the supplementary school because the fundamental proposition of human capital theory is that 'greater individual and social investments in education lead to economic benefits at both the individual and aggregate levels' (Livingstone 2002). This finding was well articulated by Mensah, who said, 'Before I was not really looking forward to go to university, but when I came here, I got a lot of help with my GCSE. And now am in college and studying to go to university.' Another interviewee, Adwoa, said that attending supplementary school definitely helped. 'I was able to use, perhaps, easier methods to those that I had been taught at mainstream school, and things that came up in the exams felt more familiar and I got excellent grades, and I am now in university, reading biological sciences.' The above assertions were further supported by a parent named Tevi, who said, 'I have seen my daughter's grades go up since she started coming to this Saturday school.' In addition to the above claim, a teacher called Edem at the supplementary school supported this claim when he reiterated that 'some students who were predicted with very low grades from their mainstream school ended up getting B grades and above as a result of early intervention and extra one-to-one support at the supplementary school and are now doing mathematics at college'.

In addition to these views about supplementary school, another teacher known as Amposah indicated that 'supplementary school attendance improves children's attainment in mainstream schools because it helps develop a better understanding of schoolwork by preparing them ahead of their mainstream mates and by creating a relaxed learning atmosphere where concepts not understood can be asked without any fear and, finally, by creating a culture of diligence in students, leading them to gain better grades at GCSE'. These positive comments expressed by students, their parents, and teachers demonstrate that there exist some sort of a positive correlation between the additional hours invested in learning at this supplementary school and the attainment and progression in the education of these migrant students. Mensah's comment is very illuminating in the sense that his perception and attitude towards learning and life changed as a result of the intervention received at the supplementary school, and now he anticipates going on further in education to a university. This change in perception and willingness to go on to university shown by Mensah is significant based on a research evidence using the National Child Development Study, which shows that the returns to an additional year of full-time education in UK are 5–6 per cent for males and 9–10 per cent for females (Dearden 2000). However, it is vital not to ignore the prevailing economic climate, which does not guarantee anyone the perceived or anticipated return of education.

Not withstanding the current economic and political climate where government subsidy for university education is being withdrawn and students are made to contribute a higher proportion towards further education, Belfield (2000) warned that with the current rates of enrolment and reduced level of public subsidy, the marginal graduate—or the individual contemplating extra education at the margin—may even face a private rate of return which is below the next best opportunity.

Conversely, the impulse of skill-based technology change may serve to validate any increases in education levels. Similarly, Checchi (2006: 7) confirms that 'almost 90 per cent of men and 80 per cent of women work in most developed countries, if they have a university degree. This contrasts 70 per cent of men and 40 per cent of men in the case of less than a compulsory education. Thus education seems to promote labour market participation and employability irrespective of gender.'

Another striking finding is that, according to the available data and report of the leadership of the supplementary school, the first cohort of the GCSE students who attended the school are all now in university apart from just one student who took a gap year to gain experience relevant to the programme she intended to pursue in university. This is consistent with the findings of the data from the Youth Cohort Study (YCS) which indicate that 'young people from minority ethnic groups are, however, much more likely than White pupils to stay on in post-compulsory education' (Pilkington 2003: 130).

This further resonated with the earlier findings by Modood which claim that 'about twice as many ethnic minority as white persons were likely to be continuing in education' (Modood 2003: 130). Interestingly, Drew also found that 'once attainment was taken into account, ethnic origin was the single most important factor in determining the chances of staying on' (Drew 2003). This led me to further examine the factors which made it possible for many of these students to move on to further education. In human capital formation, Checchi argues that 'when students are inputs in the production process, it becomes crucial to consider their individual abilities and the overall ability of the group of students. Educationalists have made clear that it is much easier (and more rewarding) to teach bright students: they understand better and more quickly raise clever questions and are typically more motivated in studying. But the converse is also true: students perform better when teachers well qualified and are motivated'.' (Checchi 2006: 85).

This is consistent with my own findings because when I asked Dodzi, 'How would you compare your teaching experience in supplementary school with mainstream school?' He gave the following answer: 'The basic difference is that students who attend supplementary school are well motivated and generally want to learn. Lower teacher-to-student ratio also favours supplementary provision. Behaviour is not a problem, and besides that, majority of the teachers are well qualified and have immense experience teaching in mainstream schools so they   are very familiar with curriculum requirements and the expectations by different exam boards.'

Nana, another well qualified teacher in both mainstream setting and the supplementary school, thinks that the reason why the children are well behaved and very keen on learning is due to the financial commitment of their parents or carers into the supplementary education programme and the school is organised and managed in terms of small class sizes which enhances personalised and individualised support and learning.

In response to a similar question posed to Adwoa, she said: 'It has definitely given me the confidence to ask more questions if I don't understand, whereas in a class of about thirty students in mainstream school, you would feel as if you are interrupting, so I would refrain from doing so.' Adwoa is not the only student who held this view. Korbla shared a similar opinion when he said, 'In supplementary school, the small class size and supportive teachers who even speak our mother tongue language and understand us easily make us feel free to ask any question we do not understand, but in my mainstream school, I sometimes feel embarrassed by my mates' response when I ask question because sometimes they think you want to be the teacher's pet.'

In an interview with the out-of-school-hours support manager called Nat in the borough where this supplementary school exists, he said that 'twenty-five out of forty-five community-led education projects are funded. Supplementary education exists to booster what already exists. If your child is doing well or not so well, you may ask, "What can I do to support them?" If you are quite rich, you can get a tutor for £30 per hour or Easter revision for £500–1000 per session. But because most communities do not have economic optional advantage, so they say, "What can we do instead of fussing and moaning about what is not being done?" They do something—participate in a supplementary school. By their very nature, they are small community-run projects, and they are not going to have thirty-odd kids in a class as is usually the case in a mainstream school has to have. It would defeat the purpose. It is about giving individualised attention to a child or group of children. And if they come to a community-run education on Saturday, then they ask the maths teacher, "How can I do this? Can I do this differently?" They get the answer and the support they need, and it is so important. It makes a difference between passing and failing, between grade A and grade B, between grade C and a grade D. It really optimises their life chances.'

My findings from the interviews of parents, teachers, and the management of the school confirm the propositions of the human capital theory in the sense that the students, by choosing to attend the supplementary school, have forgone other opportunities such as playing football, watching movies, playing computer games, or going for real or window shopping. Instead, they invest their time in extra learning. This helps them to complete their homework from mainstream school or catch up on their coursework. It also helps them to get good grades eventually and subsequently progress to higher education. The parents, on the other hand, by choosing to invest some extra money in their children's learning, hope to give them educational advantage and increase their chances of doing well in examinations. Having chosen to work on Saturdays to support these students, the teachers are already reaping the benefits of their own investments in their education. By these intervention programmes, the management are also contributing to the well-being of the society at large by promoting and moulding the future generation—another non-economic return on education.

The factors that ensured success at this site of learning are the following:

- supportive and highly motivated teachers who are well qualified and have genuine interest in the academic success of the children they teach and a dedicated leadership who are determined to see the children do well
- the willingness of some parents, despite their economic status, to go the extra mile to pay for one-to-one tuition and to give personalised support to their children at home apart from the provision on Saturday, demonstrating that the parents knowingly or unknowingly subscribe to the central thesis of the HCT
- well-motivated and driven students who are keen to learn and to attain the best possible examination results and educational goals.

One of the parents made this comment when asked, 'Why do you bring your son or daughter to this supplementary school?'

He said, 'We parents must spend time and money on the educational resources of our children. It is our responsibility to buy them books to broaden their horizon and limit the amount spent on designer clothes for our children—of course they need it but not in all fashions and colours. We must rather spend the money supplementing the education of our children because those who do that, their children do very well according to history. Those who spend money supplementing the education of their children see good results.'

Sadly, Leslie pointed out that 'unemployment is, arguably, "the major economic problem that faces the ethnic communities", with young non-white unemployment (being) particularly severe' (Leslie 2003). This is further confirmed by a Cabinet Office document report that stated that 'being from a minority ethnic background reduces people's chances of employment at all levels of qualifications' (Cabinet Office 2003).

Pilkington blames this high unemployment rate among ethnic minorities on racial discrimination, and he supported his claim by reference to the Social Exclusion Unit database which points to the fact that rates of unemployment are higher for people from minority ethnic backgrounds regardless not only of their qualification but also their place of residence, gender, and age (Cabinet Office 2003). Modood et al. further confirm this gloomy reality when they reiterated that 'among men under retirement age around 15 per cent of Whites were unemployed'.

The proportions of Chinese, African, Asians, and Indians were within the same range (9, 14, and 19 per cent respectively). By contrast, Caribbean men had an unemployment rate double that of whites (31 per cent). Black African rates, according to the census, were three times as high, and Bangladeshi and Pakistani rates were even higher at 42 and 38 per cent respectively. Female unemployment rates were generally lower than male unemployment rates. The same ethnic pattern occurs as for men, but the differences are smaller (Modood et al. 2003). These observations by Pilkington, Drew, and Modood contradict the very proposition of the HCT. However, it confirms the position held by Berthoud that 'although all minority ethnic groups face racial discrimination and poorer rate of return on educational qualifications than whites, there is no doubt that some Minority Ethnic Groups, including the Chinese, African Asians and Indians, have used the education system to improve their job prospects, while others, notably Africans, have found that their substantial investment in education has had a minimal pay off' (Berthoud 2003).

The question is, should African parents refrain from investing in their children's education in the light of these realities? The answer is no. Instead, we must recognise that education is a means to an end and a way of empowering the next generation and hence the benefits is not restricted to getting a job. We must however use the knowledge and the skills acquired to think about how we create jobs.

4.3   Application of the Social Capital Theory to the Supplementary School

The central thesis of the social capital theory can be summed in the words of Henderson and Berla when they wrote, 'When schools work together with families to support learning, children tend to succeed not just in school but throughout life. When parents are involved in their children's education at home, their children do better in school, and the schools they go to are better' (Henderson and Berla 2005).

My findings from the interviews granted to the director of the Youth Learning Network revealed that his motivation for starting the YLN was a result of his perceived lack of a sense of community and connectedness among black students, especially boys from the different parts of Africa and the Caribbean, coupled with the underachievement debate in the media.

This observation by the director resonates with Halpern, who argues that 'societies are not composed of atomised individuals. People are connected with one another through intermediate social structures- webs of association and shared understandings

GILBERT GBEDAWO

of how to behave. This social fabric greatly affects with whom, and how, we interact and co-operate. It is this everyday fabric of connection and tacit co-operation that the concept of social capital is intended to capture' (Halpern 2005: 3).

Reflecting on personal experiences as a teacher in some Inner London secondary schools where most of the students' population are black, I sometimes witness the ways this social dislocation plays out in the experiences of these children as they negotiate and interact with each other in and out of the school with utter disbelief. This apparent distrust and lack of understanding among some black children in secondary schools is a source of major concern to teachers, parents, and oftentimes students who want to learn and get an education. Could these attitudes and mind-sets be the reason for the disproportionate exclusion of black children from mainstream education as indicated earlier in the literature review? Do they suffer consequences of lacking social capital, or are they victims of racial discrimination and prejudice?

Coard (2005) argues that 'the black child's true identity is denied daily in the classroom. In so far as he is given an identity, it is a false one. He is made to feel inferior in every way. In addition to being told he is dirty and ugly and sexually unreliable.' He is told by a variety of means that he is intellectually inferior. When he prepares to leave school, and even before, he is made to realise that he and 'his kind' are only fit for manual or mental jobs.

This led Coard to conclude that the black child acquires two fundamental attitudes or beliefs as a result of experiencing the British school system: a low self-image and consequently low self-expectation in life. These are obtained through streaming, banding, bussing, ESN schools, racist news media, and a white middle class curriculum; by totally ignoring the Black child's language, history, culture, and identity. Through the choice of teaching materials, the society emphasises who and what it thinks is important, infinitesimal and irrelevant. Through the belittling, ignoring, or denial of a person's identity, one can destroy perhaps the most important aspect of a person's personality—his sense of identity, of who he is and without this (proper self-image), he will get nowhere (Coard 2005: 49).

The views from the chairman and parents agreed with Coard's sentiments and assertions. When I asked, 'What motivated you to start the supplementary school?' The chairman replied, 'The aim is to bring black children together and engage them meaningfully.' The parents affirmed this when asked why they choose to send their children to the supplementary school. These are their responses.

Aku: To give my daughter the opportunity to ask questions without feeling intimidated due to large presence of other classmates and to boost her confidence because the teachers are very good and passionate about seeing the children do well with their schoolwork.

Asantewaa: I believe in extra support for my children since they were in primary school, and I have seen the benefits of it. Also for my daughter to know that she can get extra support from a different teacher who understands her.

My view is that these parents know the benefits and rewards of learning and education but perhaps, through their own experiences, are aware about the limitations and challenges confronting teachers and students in the mainstream school setting. Their awareness gave them the impetus to act positively by sending their children to supplementary schools, where they can have a sense of belonging and unleash their potential in a supportive atmosphere.

When I asked a student called Adwoa, 'What do you like about attending supplementary school?' She responded, 'I like the fact that it teaches topics outside the national curriculum, giving us an insight into our own culture, taking us on trips, especially to trans-Atlantic slave trade museum in Bristol, the slave castles in Ghana, and other interesting places in Africa. It helps us to know more about where we come from—our heritage. I also like the motivational talks because it helps us to challenge our beliefs about our personal goals in life. I can't really say that there was anything I didn't like.'

Another student called Akorsua reiterated this when she said, 'In a way, the teachers "adopt" the students as their own children as they would like to see each one them succeed.' All the teachers want their students to do well. Likewise, all the students want to do well for their teachers, and if they achieve something, it is not only for them but for their teachers and their class.

This is Yaw's response to the same question.

Yaw: There are certain questions you might feel embarrassed in the mainstream school to ask. In a Saturday school, I can tap a teacher on the shoulder and say, 'Sir, I don't really understand this, and could you please show me how to do this again?' Anything I do not understand in the mainstream school, I write it on a list and bring it to the Saturday school so that by the time I go back next Monday, I have the answer.

The responses from students, parents, and leadership regarding the supplementary school reveal that there is a common thread that weaves together the views of the different actors in the Saturday school. The parents agree that these sites of learning provide an enabling environment where their children's confidence and self-image can be boosted, while others think that their children are valued, supported individually, and positively challenged. Others also believe that their children's voices are heard in an environment where they would not be ridiculed. According to the students, they are exposed to their own culture. Their heritage is celebrated, and their history is taught, giving them a good self-image and identity. These norms, networks, and trust generate the glue that hold them together and urge them on to succeed.

These findings are consistent with the work of Issa and Williams (2009) on complementary schools in UK. They identified four main positive factors from their study, namely:

- a curriculum that reflects the children's and the communities' experiences
- leadership by teachers who are knowledgeable about the ambitions and aspirations of the community
- experienced and qualified teachers
- small teaching groups.

These findings are also consistent with the findings of the research sponsored by the Department for Children, Schools, and Families (DCSF 2010) on the impact of supplementary schools on pupils' attainment, which include the following:

- increased confidence/self-belief/esteem
- greater motivation/interest in learning
- recognised potential and being encouraged to fulfil potential
- learning languages/cultures not taught in their mainstream schools
- higher expectations/aspirations, increased attainment, and positive teacher–parent relationships.

Now let us look at how social capital theory led to these key findings, and perhaps we will have deeper understanding of how important it is to the educational achievement and attainment of migrant children who are in UK secondary schools.

4.4 Parental Engagement and Social Capital Theory

Studies have shown that children whose parents are both physically present and attentive tend to achieve better test scores. They are more likely to complete high school and are more likely to attend college (Halpern 2005).

Throughout my interview with the parents and the teachers, I found that the participants understand and believe the crucial role parental engagement plays in the educational attainment of the black students in general and migrant students from Africa in particular. The parents noted that a positive engagement and interaction with the key stakeholders in their children's school is necessary to identify and provide the vital interventions at an early stage in the educational process of their children's learning. This can best be illustrated by the triangle shown below:

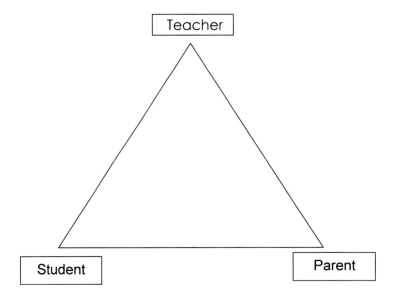

It is not enough for just the parents to interact and have a positive relationship with their child or children. It is important that the interactions between parents and teachers are positive, meaningful, engaging, and collaborative to enhance the educational attainment and achievement of the learner—in this case, the student. If there will be a breakdown of one side of the triangle above, then consequences will show up in poor behaviour, poor attendance, and inability of student to complete homework. There will be disengagement in the classroom, confrontational and defensive attitudes on the part of the various players, and subsequent underachievement of the learner due to neglect, abandonment, or exclusion from effective participation in the learning enterprise.

It is evident from my finding that sometimes there is a breakdown of this meaningful interaction and cooperation between parents and the teachers in the mainstream school as admitted by the director of the school when he said, 'The children are all different, and you must know them. Some of the challenges are not with the children but with the role of parents—parental involvement. Some parents do not have an understanding of the educational system and so find it hard to support their children. Other parents are difficult to deal with, so the schools prefer to talk to us.'

The director continued by saying, 'Some children do not have a personal ambition or goal for education. They go to school because they were driven by their situations. Education must be seen as a foundation for future economic and personal development. If you are a parent and you do not look at education that way, then there is a problem. Parents must engage with their children about what they do at school, and if there is parental neglect, this will affect the educational development of the children. One of the things we do is that we engage parents in discussions to map out what the issues are with their children's education because parents are the first educators in the world. Before the advent of formal schooling, parents are the first educators. Some of the children also have huge learning difficulties, but some African parents do not understand this. The parents may think it is labelling of their child. It is not because the child is bad but because the child may need support. We provide support by getting the mainstream schools to assess some of the children we think may have special educational needs. I got an independent agency to assess my own son, Korshi, before the school accepted that my child has a special educational need.'

Through some of these early interventions, some students with special educational needs are now on Action Plus in their mainstream schools, and it is not the child's fault. Some other children are extremely difficult, and we support them by withdrawing them and mentoring them—giving them a 'fatherly' guidance'.

Although all the parents interviewed admitted that positive relationship between them and the mainstream teachers and staff are vital for their children's educational attainment, they also admitted that as a result of other constrains (such as long hours of work, inability to personally help with their children's schoolwork, and sometimes the negative attitude of the mainstream school towards them), they are not able to foster a positive relationship.

In the case of the Ghanaian parents interviewed, language was not an issue as most of these parents speak very good English. One of the parents is a school governor in two separate schools and is very familiar with the issues of education. However, as noted by Lauglo (2000: 145), 'If the family belongs to a "visible minority" typical of those who migrated to the "North" from developing country, there is a racist exclusion which could cause outright opposition to the "white man's school" and channel immigrant youth towards a future in an ethnically distinct new "underclass". Social reproduction theory would also imply that among immigrants the principles of reproduction would broadly apply as among non-immigrants: that the relative educational success of children would mirror their family's social class and relative possession of cultural capital.'

On the basis of this, I would argue that supplementary schools, especially black supplementary schools, exist to provide the cultural and social capital necessary to facilitate the educational attainment of the 'visible minority' by acting as a bridge between mainstream schools and parents from working-class backgrounds who seem to be lacking the confidence and knowledge to engage meaningfully with the mainstream setting. The participants, especially the students, allude to this when asked the question: 'How different is the supplementary school to the school you attend?'

Adwoa: Stronger family feel to it. Everyone knows everyone.

Akua: We could ask whatever. They were teachers, helpers, parents, friends, guides, and buddies all in one.... All in three – hour lesson.

This reinforces the notion that supplementary schools act as sites for the empowerment and enrichment of positive relationships among its actors, thus building trust, responsibility, and expectations, which subsequently promote positive outcomes.

Since the aim of my research is to find out how supplementary schools contribute to the educational attainment of migrant students from Africa, it is important to ask what factors generate, nurture, and grow the social capital of the students. Because as noted by Halpern, 'At the micro-level, higher levels of child–parent contact generally lead to higher educational aspirations and attainments, but it is the quality, not just quantity of time that counts. A child's early interactions with attentive, responsive and consistent primary caregivers are critical to his or her mastering the basic social and cognitive skills on which later learning is based. Parents' social capital—support they receive from the rest of the family, their friendship networks and their relationship with the child's school—can also affect the child's educational outcome' (Halpern 2005: 167–168).

The YLN promote the social capital base of the students, teachers, and their parents by the following means:

- organisation of parental forum and motivational events
- planning and taking its members on educational trips both in the UK and Africa
- collaborating with parents to create 'learning zones' at home
- engaging parents as volunteers at the Saturday school
- forming partnership with other agencies and organisations
- establishing partnership with mainstream schools
- pastoral visits to reassure parents and families going through difficult or challenging situations such as bereavement.

When I asked the director about parental involvement and how important this is to the school, he said, 'All the directors are parents. The management team are all parents. We have parents who volunteer as well. The directors put together policies for the smooth implementation. Parents are involved in registration, making tea and also publicising to other parents. We also give references to those parents who serve as volunteers. We send some of them to trainings, and they also represent us in conference and even overseas trips.

GILBERT GBEDAWO

We also run conferences and forums for how new migrants can get involved in PTA and become governors. The agenda for the forums is to get parents involved in the life of the school, going on trips with children etc. as volunteers, and by so doing, you form partnership and also influence the decisions for the better—for example, there are cultural issues our children and staff face which may require our support. The problem with second-generation migrant is that some or most of them are becoming difficult to teach as a result of parenting issues. From experience, third- and fourth-generation migrants think the world owes them everything. Parents also think that schools are free, but schools are not free. They are sponsored by our tax money, so it is important that we as parents look at education critically. We parents have developed the sense that all our children should become engineers, doctors, etc.

Sometimes teachers ignore the cultural background of their students and think only in terms of science, English, and maths. Teachers develop the notion that black children cannot be disciplined or taught. The other thing is setting goals for our children with clear targets and boundaries. Children must be held responsible and accountable for their actions and inactions and that is the role of parents and teachers. Other reasons are, we lack black role models in our communities, nations, and internationally.

Education must make us accountable. Education is the foundation for building the future. The newly arrived migrants then can fall into the traps of these third-generation migrant due to peer pressure effect.

We need to place emphasis on the integration of our children into the right social group. Although the causes of the educational gaps are complex, I think a high percentage revolves around parenting. Fathers should play the educational role in the life of their children even though they may not be living with the mother of their children.

Parents of migrant children must spend time and money on the resources of our children's education. It is our responsibility to buy the books, broaden the horizon of our children, and stop buying only designer clothes and trainers for our children—of course they need it but not in all fashions. We should spend money supplementing the education of our children. Those who do that, their children do very well according to history. Those who spend money supplementing the education of their children see good results. Education must be broad and children must be encouraged to learn musical instruments and write music. Parents must be persistent with the learning of their children, support them, encourage them, and set targets for them, then they can and would achieve.'

4.5 Conclusion

In conclusion, this chapter has used human capital theory and social capital theory to analyse the experiences of students within supplementary school and the parts played by teachers, parents, and the leadership of the supplementary school towards the educational attainment of migrant students, especially those from Africa.

My findings reveal that, generally, the students' experiences with supplementary schools are positive, meaningful, and enriching, and they make an impact on their mainstream work and subsequent attainment in their GCSE examinations, although the extent of this impact cannot be quantified. It is clear that the contributions of supplementary schools towards migrant students' education are vital and go beyond just getting good grades in examinations.

Parental involvement in the supplementary schools, dedicated and motivated teachers, and visionary leadership exhibited by the management are major determinants of the ongoing success stories of the students who participate in them.

Within the confines of the available evidence from the collected data, it is clear that the role and the contributions of supplementary schools are vital to the achievement of the Every

GILBERT GBEDAWO

Child Matters agenda by the UK government and the Millennium Development Goals but, most importantly, towards closing the attainment gap between ethnic minorities and their white counterparts.

CHAPTER 5

Conclusions and Recommendations

5.1 Introduction

This chapter summarises the key findings of the study by revisiting the experiences of the students, the role parents play in the education of migrant students from Africa, and how supplementary schools contribute toward the educational attainment of the students who participate in them. It ends with some recommendations.

5.2 Summary

This research was about the contributions of supplementary schools to the educational attainment of migrant children from Africa and the parental contribution to their schooling in the United Kingdom.

Black supplementary schools started over four decades ago in response to the apparent racial discrimination experienced by black children in British mainstream schools, and they were intended to be sites where the true identity and personality of black children can be restored and celebrated. They were also intended to be places of solace from the racial discrimination and prejudice experienced in mainstream schools by engaging black children in extra lessons aimed at addressing the underachievement they face in their mainstream schools. Another main focus was to expose black children to black history and black role models to help them have a positive self-image and identity and take pride in themselves.

Lately, supplementary schools have increased across the UK, and their contribution to the educational attainment, especially of migrant communities, have been noted by some local authorities. Recently, the government of the UK has officially acknowledged their impact and is seeking to regulate and further enhance their activity through the establishment of the National Resource Centre for supplementary schools.

It was clear in the literature review that, although they have been in existence for close to half a century, there is limited research on them, so I set out to find out the experiences of the students who attend them, the contributions they make towards the educational outcome of migrant students from Africa, and how parents are involved in them. Although there is no single supplementary school solely dedicated to African students. I chose to investigate this group because of shared cultural heritage and because of my keen interest in supporting and helping students to become successful in their education.

The literature reviewed indicates that there are gaps in the educational attainment between migrant students and the white majority, and the reasons were explored. Migrant students from Africa, like many other migrant students and ethnic minorities, face certain challenges that are unique to them in schools and in the labour market.

The social and human capital theories were deployed to help us understand how supplementary schools address the educational disadvantage of migrant students and position them to achieve academic excellence in the mainstream schools they attend.

5.3 Research Questions Revisited

My methodology was qualitative and I interviewed the participants. The data analysis used was to triangulate and validate the findings. In the interview, I was looking for the following information:

1. What are the experiences of migrants in the supplementary schools they attend?
2. How different is the supplementary schools from the mainstream school?
3. What are the motivations of parents for sending their children to supplementary schools?
4. What are the parents' experiences of supplementary school and the mainstream school that their children attend?
5. How are parents involved in supplementary schools?
6. How does attendance of supplementary school affect students' attainment in mainstream school?

5.4 Research Findings

The findings based on the interviews, document analysis and the literature revealed the following:

1. Migrant students who attend supplementary school are motivated to achieve and enjoy the time they spent at this sites of learning with support from parents and carers.
2. Supplementary schools foster social cohesion and a sense of community among migrant students who attend, which makes a positive impact on their sense of identity.
3. Supplementary school attendance helps the students to get additional support with their mainstream work, positioning them to better understand their subjects and subsequently positioning them to excel in their examination.
4. Supplementary schools play key roles in the integration of Migrant students into secondary schools in the United

Kingdom and help their parents to better understand the UK education system and how it functions.

5. Partnership between supplementary schools and mainstream schools could be mutually beneficial and enhance the education of migrant students.

6. Parents tend to be more engaged with supplementary schools than the mainstream schools due to their very nature.

7. Quality parental involvement with the schooling of migrant students enhances their educational aspiration and attainment.

8. The small class sizes, well-qualified and passionate teachers, supportive parents, and strong leadership at supplementary schools make a huge difference to the outcomes of the students who attend.

5.5 Conclusion

My study has shown that the need for supplementary schools as sites for the educational and holistic development of black migrant students today in UK secondary schools is as important as when Coard made the call for their establishment over thirty-five years ago.

In their attempt to provide decent education for their children, migrant parents and ethnic minorities are confronted with daunting challenges, ranging from institutional racism to low expectation on the part of the teachers who regard black children as underachievers and displaying difficult behavioural tendencies which make them difficult to teach, thus leading to a disproportionate rate of exclusion from school. These migrants also face harsh treatment in the labour market as a result of discrimination and are likely to find themselves working two or sometimes more jobs to keep the family going.

However, realising the key role education plays in enhancing one's future prospects and social standing, these parents resort to supplementary education to booster the chances of their children's educational success.

These supplementary schools seem to be doing well, considering the limited resources available to them. Parents are the main source of funding they receive, although some receive some sort of funding from the LA in which they are situated. Considering the immense contributions they are making to the educational aspiration and the attainment of migrant children, I would like to make the following recommendations:

1. Mainstream schools should make their premises available for use especially at weekends to facilitate the work of these schools as this will be mutually beneficial to the overall educational attainment of the children.
2. More funding should be made available to pay for the services of quality teachers in supplementary schools.
3. There should be some sort of ongoing monitoring of supplementary schools to provide accountability.
4. More research on the impact of supplementary school attendance and educational attainment of migrant students is needed to evaluate the work of supplementary schools.

As rightly observed by Issa and Williams, 'Complementary schools are organic to their communities. Teachers and parents share an understanding of racism. Being themselves part of ethnic minority communities, the teachers are uniquely placed to know how racism operates in schools and how children and their parents experience it' (Issa and Williams 2009: 141). It is therefore imperative that schools, black parents, children, leaders, and those individuals and organisations who genuinely seek to promote the educational excellence of all children galvanise their resources in a synergistic manner because, indeed, every child matters.

CHAPTER 6

The Role of Students towards Educational Excellence

It is possible to become an A* student when you understand the processes involved in moving from average to excellence. The main purpose of this book is to share with students and readers like you who desire to succeed in education and learning how to achieve that and become all that they desire and hope for. My experience of two decades of teaching prompted me to show all those who desire educational excellence the way to achieve it.

Recent GCSE exam results in England attracted a lot of media attention as majority of the students received a D grade instead of a C grade due to the raising of the grade boundaries. A lot of students became angry due to a perceived injustice by the exam boards as their counterparts who wrote the same exams in January managed to get C grade with the same mark. In the light of all these failures to obtain a pass grade, there were also other students who had ten A* and three A grades in the same exam.

Some of these students with straight As happen to attend the same schools with those who felt cheated by the exam regulatory boards. Should anyone settle for average if there is a possibility of achieving the best outcome?

The main concern is what lessons we can learn from those who performed brilliantly in their exams in order to emulate these higher achievers of educational success. After all, there are lessons we can all learn even from seemingly small things like the ants as noted in Proverbs 6:6.

> Go to the ant, thou sluggard: consider her ways and be wise.

Wisdom demands that we carefully observe those who are excelling in their work so that we can learn from them, thereby positioning ourselves to replicate their success or better still achieve higher. This is the reason why I write this book, to guide you systematically on your journey towards educational excellence and glory.

My hope is that, as you decide to leave the rut of average by studying the principles and laws outlined in the pages of this book, your days of contentment with average results is over. A new door shall be opened to you, leading you into the glorious destiny reserved for those who apply themselves to the laws and principles that govern and regulate uncommon success.

Sooner or later, you will be glad that you have read and studied these principles because they will guarantee your success.

Why Are You in School?

The purpose of education or schooling is the acquisition of knowledge. The knowledge acquired is powerful enough to shape, develop, and strengthen your skills and change the way you think. Knowledge, when properly directed, applied, and utilised, can determine how far you will go in life and who you will ultimately become. That is why many people say knowledge is power although it is the knowledge that is understood and applied correctly that makes an enormous difference. It is important therefore to understand the reason why we go to school because if this is not properly understood, then it is most likely that we will not maximise the opportunities that we are given through the various agencies in the school designed to help shape and mould our innate desires, aspirations, goals, dreams, and ultimately, destiny.

The various aspects of schooling could be compared to the pressure which is applied to an ordinary carbon to change its state from an undesirable element to a sought-after gem called the diamond. Sometimes the heat may be unpleasant during the purification process of most metal ores; however, this is crucial to separate the impurities from the desired product. Schooling and education are necessary to bring the best out of every child and learner, and a great importance must be attached to this since the knowledge acquired through studying is vital in making us useful citizens, workers, friends, men, women, leaders, neighbours, boys, and girls.

Those who deliberately ignore education and knowledge forfeit the chance to develop their capacity to manage, contribute, and lead in the various aspects of life, whether it is musical, entertainment, sports, educational, social, economic, political, and religious.

In Hosea 4:6, it is noted: 'My people are destroyed for lack of knowledge. Because thou hast rejected knowledge, I will also reject thee, that thou shalt be no priest to me: Since you have forgotten the law of your God, I also will forget your children.'

Malachi 2:7 declares: 'For the lips of a priest ought to preserve knowledge, and from his mouth men should seek instruction—because he is the messenger of the LORD Almighty.'

Those who reject knowledge deny themselves the opportunity to become key players in the affairs of life. The protégé of Moses, Joshua as documented in the scripture was admonished to study and meditate on the laws day and night in order to become successful.

In Joshua 1:8, it is stated: 'This book of the law shall not depart out of thy mouth; but thou shalt meditate therein day and night, that thou might observe to do according to all that is written therein: for then though shalt make thy way prosperous, and then thou shalt have good success.'

Knowledge acquisition, I argue, is an important contributory factor towards a successful outcome in any enterprise of life; therefore, every step should be taken to acquire, retain, and use knowledge appropriately. School attendance or education is a means to an end. That end for some is banking, politics, medicine, teaching, plumbing, catering, management, mining, aviation, engineering, information technology, and the list goes on. In view of this, you must make every effort to invest the present in the pursuit of knowledge. This will position you to seize any opportunity the future presents for leadership, growth and development because the future belongs to those who prepare for it today.

When you make up your mind that your future must and should be greater than your present, then it is imperative that you take responsibility for your knowledge acquisition by regarding your teachers as facilitators of knowledge—those who open the gates of knowledge and show you the beautiful cities of discoveries that await your exploration.

The first step is to value, respect, and dignify any opportunity you have to interact with them. This will position you to receive instructions to help you discover new knowledge and guidance. These interactions and associations are most likely to affect your intellectual and academic development even though other aspects of your life may be affected in a good and a better way.

I surmise that your overall development depends on the level of intellectual enrichment and your ability to cultivate and grow in knowledge and wisdom. This is the reason why you attend school; therefore, you must see every opportunity as a learning opportunity and your teachers as facilitators of this knowledge.

We have established the purpose of schooling and the importance of knowledge, however, what type of knowledge does one then need to focus on?

GILBERT GBEDAWO

As a foundation, all the relevant bodies of knowledge offered in your primary and secondary school are essential. When you start sixth form or college then you can narrow down on specific subjects which are appropriate for your unique talents, skillset, interests, vocation and calling. Indeed one must also strive to add new areas of interest such as, learning to play a musical instrument, joining the school choir or participating in any other extracurricular activities. These are vital for holistic development and full expression of your particular area of talents or abilities. These areas are equally necessary as it will help you unlock your full potential.

This is where parental support and involvement is crucial because a synergic relationship between schools and parents will go a long way to support each and every learner to reach their full potential. This may be time-consuming, but hold on! The time invested properly in nurturing the seeds of greatness in a child in a loving manner will someday bring a good harvest that may far exceed our imagination. Those parents or guardians who may not be able to do this must act early to seek support because nature hates vacuum. The breakdown in the support system may be detrimental to the child as they may go in search of other ways to be engaged, which can be counterproductive. Idleness become the breeding ground for all sorts of vices, so let us rise up to the challenges of parenthood, and if we do, then we play our role in contributing towards the educational excellence of that child, positioning him or her on the path of distinction.

My prayer for you as a parent is that the wisdom necessary to do this will come to you and the ability to rise to the situation will be supplied so that your child will become an A* student in an environment where the majority are settling for the average grades.

My earnest desire for you reading this book as a student is that you will be able to respect and honor the efforts of your parents, guardian and teachers so that every investment in your learning will be rewarded with excellent results.

I trust that, as you read carefully the remaining pages of this book, your paths will continue to shine and the insights needed to shine as a student and a learner will be given to you by the Almighty God, who is the source of all knowledge and wisdom but uses our earthly teachers and parents as conduits to shape our lives and destinies.

Let me now address the opening question posed in the title: 'Why am I in school?' Firstly, allow me to elucidate the meaning of school. According to *Collins English Dictionary*, 'school' is 'an institution or building at which children and young people usually under the age of 19 receive education'. Another definition for 'school' is 'a place or a sphere of activity that instructs'. A third concept of 'school' is 'a body of people or pupils adhering to a certain set of principles, doctrines, or methods'.

We can therefore conclude that the purpose of a school is to receive education and instruction and to adhere to certain principles, doctrines, or methods of doing things.

Education, in its general sense, is a form of learning in which knowledge, skills, and habits of a group of people are transferred from one generation to the next through teaching, training, research, or simply through autodidacticism—that is, learning on your own. Generally, it occurs through any experience that has a formative effect on the way one thinks, feels, or acts.

Etymologically, the word 'education' is derived from the Latin *educatio*, which means 'a breeding, a bringing up, or a rearing'. This is related to the homonym *educo*, meaning, 'I lead forth, I take out, I raise up, or I erect'.

Wikipedia, however, noted that the individual purposes for pursuing education can vary. However, in early age, the focus is generally around developing basic interpersonal communication and literacy skills in order to further one's ability to learn more complex skills and subjects. After acquiring these basic abilities, education is commonly focused towards individuals' gaining necessary knowledge and skills to improve their ability to create value and livelihood for themselves. Satisfying personal curiosities and the desire for personal development to better oneself without career-based reasons for doing so are also common reasons why people pursue education and use schools.

In my view, the fundamental purpose of education is to prepare individuals to be able to harness their innate abilities (whether intellectual, emotional, or spiritual), to think constructively and creatively, and to apply these thoughts to solve problems, thus making the world a better place for humanity and all other flora and fauna species.

In Genesis 1:28, it says:

> And God blessed them, and God said unto them, be fruitful, and multiply, and replenish the earth, and subdue it: and have dominion over the fish of the sea, and over the fowl of the air, and over every living thing that moveth upon the earth.

In addition, Genesis 2:15 states: 'And the LORD God took the man, and put him into the Garden of Eden to dress it and to keep it.'

Wisdom key 1: whatever you are not willing to dress, you cannot keep.

The purpose of education, therefore, is to receive instruction to make our world a better place for all. However, let us also consider what others say about education. Perhaps we might learn a lesson or two from them.

> The aim of education should be to teach us rather how to think, than what to think- rather to improve our minds, so as to enable us think for ourselves, than to load the memory with thoughts of other men. (Bill Beattie)

> The whole purpose of education is to turn mirrors into windows. (Sydney J. Harris)

STEPS TOWARDS EDUCATIONAL EXCELLENCE

Education is what remains after one has forgotten what one has learned in school. (Albert Einstein)

If you think education is expensive try ignorance. (Andy McIntyre and Derek Bok)

To the uneducated, an A is just three sticks. (A. A. Milne)

The object of education is to prepare the young to educate themselves throughout their lives. (Robert Maynard Hutchins)

He, who opens a school door, closes a prison. (Victor Hugo)

Education is a progressive discovery of our ignorance. (Will Durant)

A child educated only at school is an educated child. (George Santayana)

Education's purpose is to replace an empty mind with an open one. (Malcolm S. Forbes)

Education is an ornament in prosperity and a refuge in adversity. (Aristotle)

Education is the ability to listen to almost anything without losing your temper or your self-confidence. (Robert Frost)

It is the mark of an educated mind to be able to entertain a thought without accepting it. (Aristotle)

Education is the movement from darkness to light. (Allan Bloom)

Education is not preparation for life; education is life itself. (John Dewey)

GILBERT GBEDAWO

> Education is the transmission of civilization. (Ariel and Will Durant)

Let us conclude these quotes by reminding ourselves by the words of Walker Percy: 'You can get all A's and still flunk life.'

Another reason why I am writing this book is to show students that they can continually remain A* students in school and later in life because education is a process and rightly so. It is a means to an end and not an end in itself. My hope and prayer is that students will continue to nurture the seeds of greatness in them through the acquisition of practical knowledge which is designed to make their lives glorious and beautiful as they embark on their assignments and instructions to live in a better world than they inherited.

Remember the words of Solomon in Proverbs 4:18:

> But the path of the just is as the shining light, that shineth more and more unto the perfect day.

I declare that you also will arise and shine from now onwards!

> I arise and shine for my light is come and the glory of the Lord rises upon me. (Isaiah 60:1)

CHAPTER 7

Seven Predictable Behaviours of Outstanding Students

The first question I would like to address here is who at all is an outstanding or A* student?

1. The A* student is, first of all, an uncommon learner who is motivated and driven by the desire to become the best in the subjects being taught.
2. An A* student is also the student who goes the extra mile to complete all required tasks and, in the process, discovers new methods and knowledge.
3. An A* student is a high achiever who is never satisfied with average results but knows that the buck stops with him or her.
4. The A* student is an active participant in the teaching–learning process.
5. The A* student loves books, seeks knowledge, and respects those who are guiding and teaching him or her.
6. The A* student is never afraid to ask questions but uses questions as an opportunity to learn and understand further what is being taught.
7. The A* student also belongs to a study group and uses the library often for research and collective or independent learning.

8. The A* student is also the learner who is well organised and has an effective knowledge-retrieval system in place.
9. The A* student also has a timetable and organises his or her time effectively around it but he or she also knows when and how to refresh him or herself by engaging in extracurricular activities, whether it is sports, music, or other forms of hobbies.
10. Finally, an A^ student scores over 95 percent almost every time in almost every exam.

If that sounds like you, then praise God, hallelujah! But if not, remember that all things are possible unto those who believe. Just have faith and use your faith to start the process of reaching the A* status because you are the reason why I write this book and you will rise as you decide beginning from this moment that you can do everything through Christ, who strengthens you. Receive strength from above, and do what must be done even now.

Let us now examine the seven habits or predictable behavioural patterns of those who become A* students, and you are the next person to attain this status.

Behaviour 1
Respect and Keeping to Time Always

They develop and use a lesson timetable at school and at home—public and private. They wake up the same time, go to school the same time, study the same time, play the same time, and go to bed the same time. They have a pattern of behaviour that is predictable.

> Successful people do daily what the unsuccessful do occasionally. (Dr Mike Murdock)

The fact remains that your respect of time is a prediction of how successful you will become in your examinations and in life afterwards.

STEPS TOWARDS EDUCATIONAL EXCELLENCE

Think about very successful individuals you know or celebrate. They all have one thing in common. They have a watch on their wrists. One of my mentors usually says that he has never seen a successful person without a watch. It is amazing how developed nations always have big watches displayed in public places, but when you visit developing nations, you will seldom see watches in public places. Also, majority of the people in those nations have less regard for timekeeping and punctuality to both private and public functions.

My dear students, if you are going to succeed in your education and with your studies, it is vital that you start to respect time and begin to make the most out of every waking time you have. The only commodity we have in common is the time available to us when we are up. We all have twenty-four golden hours as gift to us, but the most important thing is what we do with the gift of time. Do we make the most of it, or do we waste it on unnecessary and irrelevant undertakings? My prayer for you is that you will start to invest your time wisely in your studies and towards personal development of your gifts and talents.

Overexposure to today's media platforms has caused a catastrophic mismanagement of time and resources. Surprisingly, much can be accomplished when one chooses how they use their time.

An unbalanced lifestyle is detrimental to one's mental well-being, which in turn affects one's ability to produce meaningful results in the future. Consider the words of King Solomon:

> To everything there is a season, and a time to every purpose under the heaven: A time to be born, and a time to die; a time to plant, and a time to pluck up that which is planted. (Ecclesiastes 3:1–2)

The question is, do you know what you must be doing in this season of your life? Do you have an understanding of the purpose of being in school? Why are you in school? Why do you go from one lesson to another lesson? Why do you do what you are doing or going to do? It is vital to have a goal for each day.

If you can discern the importance of the moments you have, then you can maximise them and become the best student and an uncommon achiever in school, at home, and subsequently in life. Do not waste your time, but instead, choose to become better by wisely investing your time because, surely, a time of reward is coming based on whatever you have invested. If you do not have a watch on your wrist, then you can start from there. Buy a watch and wear it at all times so you can keep track of how you use the golden opportunities that life presents in a form of time.

Behaviour 2
A* Students Honour the Advice of Their
Parents, Teachers and Mentors

Precious reader, let me remind you, though it may not seem so, your parents have your best interests at heart. When you honor and dignify the positive counsel that they give you, you have the opportunity to learn from their mistakes and experiences thus avoiding circumstances that may derail you. Most parents want the very best for their children because children carry the DNA of their parents. Children come from and are extension of their parents, and hence, most parents will guide and steer their children towards success.

However, it is up to you to work with your parents, your teachers at school, or your mentors to realise your full potential and become an outstanding student.

Parents oftentimes have been to the future you are trying to get to, and they can, from their experience, tell you what can accelerate your success. Some of these experiences may be as a result of unpleasant memories from the past, however, they are knowledgeable about matters relating to life, which you may find useful. I am sure that you are better off when you listen to their counsel and work with them on your way to unleashing the success you so crave and desire.

STEPS TOWARDS EDUCATIONAL EXCELLENCE

A mentor of mine often says that there are two ways we learn: through experiences or through your mentors. Personal experiences may be a costly and a difficult way of learning. But when you work with your mentors, then your success can be accelerated, and you can realise your true potential.

I am a great tennis fan. I like to watch Venus and Serena Williams. They epitomise what can be achieved when you are surrounded by positive parents who model success through sheer belief, persistence, perseverance, and willingness to sacrifice the present so that the next generation can be better off. Such parents deserve respect and honour, and if you are going to succeed in life, you must choose the path of honour, especially of your parents and/or those who are investing knowledge, energy, and experience to make you a better person.

Recently, when Serena won the Australian Open, she remarked that she was not born into a rich family; however, her parents are spiritually rich and supportive and have contributed in a way towards her success.

> Honour your father and your mother, so that you may live long in the land the LORD your God is giving you. (Exodus 20:12)

> Honour your father and mother. This is the first commandment with a promise. (Ephesians 6:2)

It is sad to see how some young people with great potential choose to waste their lives through dishonour and bad external influences. The recent events of young people choosing a culture of violence, disregarding the sacredness of human life, mean that parents must and should take responsibility and teach their children about importance of honoring people. Many of those incarcerated chose a path of dishonor, violence and disobedience. My sincerest hope is that your child will not be a victim of the ills of society, particularly gang culture; instead may they aspire to follow a path of respect and dignity to honor both you and others.

Behaviour 3
A* Students Have a Sense of Purpose and Discipline

The key to success is identifying the purpose for whatever you do. When you discover the purpose behind your studies, then and only then would you be able to maximise the opportunities you have as a learner.

Outstanding students always have a sense of purpose, whether they are in class, in the library, or by themselves. They are independent learners who are well organised. They know exactly what they want out of their time in school. They are determined to succeed and work diligently and assiduously towards their goals. They have a written goal and keep track of their time by investing in a planner. They make notes in a lesson and keep a timetable. They know the examination boards of the subjects they are studying. They strive to improve on their performance and become better. These students invest in textbooks and additional learning resources. They oftentimes have an outline of the programmes of study or syllabus. They engage in extracurricular activities and use the playtime to relax and get rejuvenated.

In my twenty years as a teacher, I have taught, mentored, and coached outstanding students, and they have common traits. They put in the hours necessary to succeed. They ask questions and go to the library to research and find out things for themselves. They believe that success is 1 per cent inspiration and 99 per cent perspiration, so they go the extra mile and study hard.

> Do you see someone skilled in their work? They will serve before kings, they will not serve before officials of low rank. (Proverbs 22:29)

Uncommon students have 'I can' attitude towards their learning and studies. They hope the best and make every effort to put the very best into their work.

> I can do all things through him who strengthens me. (Philippians 4:13)

These uncommon students do not complain when challenged, but they believe that if it has to be done, it has to be done to the best of their abilities.

Behaviour 4
A* Students Have a Positive Attitude
towards Learning and Education

Attitudes determine your placement in life. May I take this one level up? Your attitude towards learning will determine the grades you will obtain in your examinations. Exceptional students maintain a positive attitude and demonstrate that by being willing to take on new challenges and ask questions to seek clarification. They are willing to use every opportunity as a learning experience to enhance their performance and productivity. It is absolutely great to have a high IQ and be gifted; however, it is mainly your attitude that will sustain you at the peak of excellence and performance.

The attitude you display will either attract the right people to help make your dreams and goals come to pass or attract the wrong friends who will waste your time, energy, and resources and derail you from greater achievements.

Attitude is crucial in any given outcome. The attitude of perseverance, endurance, thoughtfulness, and hard work ensures a successful outcome in any enterprise. Some people complain and grumble about everything life offers. Those people have already set the barrier to their personal and individual achievements. These people see only the negative in any given situation, but there is a group of people who choose the pathway of distinction and excellence. These people stay focused. They refuse to give up irrespective of the challenges they confront while learning or working on a given task. These students use their energy to solve problems and seek better ways of doing things. They refuse to become part of the status quo.

Like eagles, they mount up with the wings of determination and soar to the higher grounds of success and victory. These students believe that they can do all things. They believe that all things are possible. They hope against hope and use every situation as a learning opportunity. These students have the desire to succeed and organise their time around the desire through effective planning. Uncommon students know why they are in school and maximise their time while there by extracting knowledge from every learning opportunity.

Behaviour 5
A* Students Are Well Organised

One of the hallmarks of A* students is the way they prepare ahead of every teaching and learning experience. They prepare physically by the way they dress for learning. They prepare mentally by displaying a positive mental attitude. They prepare spiritually by believing that they can do all things through Christ, who is the source of their strength. And they prepare emotionally by being present in the moment and avoiding the tendency of daydreaming. They organise their learning resources well by acquiring the right tools and equipment. They invest in themselves by buying the right textbooks, exercise books, graph books, and calculators. They also invest in information-retrieval systems, like a tablet or a laptop. They keep diaries and have a timetable. They know the programme of study and what is expected of them. They are knowledgeable of the various requirements expected of them by examination boards of the subjects they wish to study. They are very familiar with past examination questions and make every effort to practise outside of the classroom.

They know and understand their areas of strength and weakness and are never shy to ask for help.

These students understand that proper preparation prevents poor performance, so they organise themselves and work out every detail of their plans through dedication, commitment, and maintaining focus till the task is accomplished to the best of their ability. This set them apart from the average students, who are satisfied with the status quo.

How then do you become organised?

Let us start from your personal appearance. Start by taking time to dress smartly before leaving for school because if you look smart, you will soon find out that it improves your personal self-image, esteem, and confidence, and you can then translate that to your schoolwork.

The second area to pay attention to is the organisation of your school bag. Make sure you have the right books and pieces of equipment in your school bag—the right pens, pencils, mathematical set, graph books, a calculator, and tracing papers.

There is no point in investing a lot of money in your physical appearance and ignoring the most important part, which is your mind. I highly recommend that you invest in textbooks and other learning resources that will facilitate your understanding of the subjects being taught at school. What about your school or community library? Go borrow books and study them.

Learn to prioritise your time by developing a learning timetable, and use it always. Diaries are important, and you must invest in it and use it. Write down clearly your daily goals every day in order of importance. Work out your daily goals, and tick them off as you accomplish a particular task.

Remember, great things come in small packages, so take time to accomplish those small daily goals, and before you know it, you are accomplishing major tasks that will improve and drive you towards greater success and achievement.

There is a Chinese adage that says, 'A journey of a thousand miles starts with one step.' Take that one step today, and seize the moment. Make hay while the sun shines. Strike while the iron is hot. Redeem the time. Go for it. Organise your time, and derive the maximum benefit from every hour, knowing that today is all you have, tomorrow is in the womb, and yesterday is in the tomb. It is gone! Forever gone! Work today, and live in the moment. Do your very best! Give it all you have before the day ends.

GILBERT GBEDAWO

Live each day as if it is your last day on earth, and accomplish great things. Let no one rob you of the precious gift of time—that is all we have to accomplish greater success and graduate top of the class with distinction. It takes hard work and dedication, but it can be done, so do it!

When you begin to taste the fruits of dedication and success, you will always want more success as success breeds success, so start today by focusing your attention on the subject that you find challenging. Do not leave it till the last minute. It will surprise you that when you begin to focus your mind on understanding these seemingly hard subjects, all of a sudden a light begins to shine in the darkness. Step by step, you overcome the obstacles and start to shine.

Behaviour 6
A* Students Are Self-Motivated

Motivation can be both intrinsic and extrinsic. The former comes from within the individual, and the latter is externally generated by those around the individual. These people may be parents, classmates, teachers, and other support groups that the individual (or in our case, the student) may be exposed to.

Motivation, whether it is intrinsic or extrinsic, is crucial for outstanding performance. Those who are motivated to succeed in school will overcome every obstacle towards their personal learning and growth.

All outstanding students share this trait. They galvanise the support, advice, and the experiences of those who have gone before them and use it to succeed. They are driven by the quest and the desire to achieve and fulfil their personal best. They can visualise the outcome of hard work and determination. They know and use their imagination to capture the very future they want to create through studies.

Motivated students understand the importance of personal commitment through self-discipline and determination. They hold themselves accountable ultimately for the achievement of their written goals.

They do not indulge in a culture of blaming others for their situations, but instead, they hold themselves responsible for where they are in their journey.

It is always important to stay motivated by engaging in activities that enables you to have a positive mental attitude and fortitude. Some of these activities may include but not limited to the following:

1. The prayer hour
   Prayer is a powerful force which positions an individual to have a dialogue with the Almighty God. It is a moment where we can ask our heavenly Father for strength to overcome any impending challenge or simply the inner strength to see a task to its completion. It may be a time to ask for wisdom to know how to go about your day or your studies. The Holy Scripture encourage us always to pray and not to faint or give up.

2. Listening to motivational or faith-building messages or music
   There is a tremendous power in hearing the word of God. It builds your faith and releases inner strength to help you carry out your daily routines. It also guides you in the right direction and prevents you from joining wrong people or following the wrong advice from peers. Listening to the Word of God increases your wisdom, and with wisdom, you can achieve whatever you set your eyes on.

3. Writing down your daily goals
   When you start a day with a clear set of smart goals which are well written in order of importance, then and only then can you be sure that you will achieve them. When your goals are written, then you will have the motivation to work on the tasks you have assigned yourself till you complete them. There is joy in completing those goals, and it gives you a sense of achievement.

GILBERT GBEDAWO

When you do this over weeks and over months, then you are on the way to become an uncommon achiever. This is what sets you apart from the crowd and qualifies you to become a successful student capable of achieving A* grades in all subjects. This is possible, and you can do it.

Behaviour 7
A* Students Engage in Some Form of Physical Exercise

A healthy mind lives and thrives in a healthy body. It is important to stay healthy through the discipline of physical exercise. This will make you fit and give you the much-needed endurance to accomplish tasks. It will also improve your mental and physical alertness especially during learning and in school settings.

Most of the outstanding students I have taught enjoy and participate in at least one sport or recreational activity. This is vital as it helps them learn team-building skills and, at the same time, develop competitive edge. There is a joy in winning as a team or being part of the winning team. The skills of endurance, training, determination, and discipline that are developed in such sporting activities can be transferred to learning zones.

A paper presented by Felfe et al. (2001) indicated that there are positive effects of participation in sports on children's skills. Overall, school grades and non-cognitive skills improve substantially, where the latter effect is mainly driven by a reduction in emotional problems and peer problems. These findings are supported by the fact that children who engage in sports also fare better in terms of health and general well-being.

In addition, it is well documented that through participation in sports and physical education, young people learn the importance of key values, such as honesty, teamwork, fair play, respect for themselves and others, and adherence to rules.

Finally, sports provide the forum for young people to learn how to deal with competition and how to cope with both winning and losing (www.sportsanddev.org).

It is my hope that as you practise these seven behaviours, you will stand out and become a meaningful achiever in your school and, indeed, in your community. I trust and pray that you become a student of distinction and excellence through diligence and determination.

The Lord bless your efforts and crown your work with good success in the name of Jesus Christ. Let me share Vanessa Odunsi's journey towards educational excellence with you in the hope that it will motivate both students and parents to work together to achieve success in collaboration with both the mainstream school and supplementary schools.

Towards Educational Excellence: The Journey of Vanessa Odunsi

My name is Vanessa Odunsi, and I am currently a 19-year-old student entering my second year at UCL (University College London), where I am studying BA German and Latin.

My earliest memory of primary education was going for an intake exam at my independent primary school. Prior to this point, my parents had realised that I was extremely bright and was very competent in English and maths in comparison to other children in my age group. Therefore, they wanted to place me in a challenging environment where I would constantly be mentally stimulated. My parents always put my education first and enrolled me into an independent primary school. I always say that my primary school, Eastcourt Independent School, gave me the best foundation in terms of my work ethic and attitude towards learning. I had homework every day and had to complete some reading with a parent from the age of four. By year 1, I was choosing my own books and reading independently. This ignited my passion for reading, and from an early age, I became an avid reader, particularly of Jacqueline Wilson and the Harry Potter series. As a result, I became more interested in creative writing and English literature. My parents would always take me to the library to borrow books, and as I became older, I began purchasing books myself and grew quite a collection. During the summer holidays, my parents made a point of taking me and my siblings out to the

GILBERT GBEDAWO

National History Museum and the Science Museum, which we really enjoyed.

When I was in year 4, my parents began preparing me for my 11+ entrance examinations into secondary school. I attended supplementary school on Saturdays and attended the crash courses in verbal and non-verbal reasoning during the school holidays. I was successful in achieving my place at Chelmsford County High School for Girls (CCHS), my first choice, and I placed thirteenth out of the 600+ girls who had sat the exam. I also took the Brentwood School entrance exam and was called for a scholarship interview because I had scored in the top percentile. I was successful in achieving a 50 per cent scholarship; however, I turned down the offer in favour of taking my place at CCHS.

At CCHS, my love for learning grew exponentially. I was exposed to new subjects and innovative methods of learning. From year 7, I was learning three languages (French, German, and Latin) as well as humanities and technology (woodwork, electronics, and textiles). During my time in the lower school (years 7–9), I was able to explore various subjects and find aspects which I really enjoyed and wanted to pursue further. At this point in my education, I realised that I had a talent for learning languages and excelled in my classes. In year 9, I completed my first GCSE in information and communication technology (ICT) and achieved an A*. In this year, I was also able to choose my GCSE options (aside from the core/compulsory subjects: maths, English language, English literature, biology, chemistry, and physics), which were drama, French, German, Latin, physical education, and religious studies. I had always performed well at school, but it was when I was in the upper school (years 10–11) that I realised that this was the time that really mattered, and I was determined to achieve the best grades possible. CCHS is also a grammar school, so there was a significant emphasis on achieving one's potential and exceeding expectations. I worked extremely hard, and with the support of my parents and Mr Gilbert Gbedawo, who gave me additional tuition in maths, biology, chemistry, and physics in August 2012, I achieved ten A*s and three As in my GCSEs.

During the summer before moving up to the sixth form, I decided that I wanted to make some money for myself, and I became a personal tutor. I taught English, maths, German, French, and Latin to students who were struggling at school or who wanted to advance themselves ahead of their syllabus in preparation for the upcoming academic year. I did this independently and gained a whole cohort of students through word of mouth of family friends and church members. I also worked for a family friend who runs her own 11+ tuition centre, and I was the sole additional teacher for verbal and non-verbal reasoning, maths, and English. I still work as a part-time tutor in the summer holidays both for myself and for the tuition centre.

I decided to stay at CCHS for sixth form as I knew that it was the best place for me to achieve my potential and to apply to the top universities. I studied German, Latin, economics, English literature, and general studies at AS level, and I also took an international baccalaureate diploma in Italian. I took these subjects because I knew that I wanted to go on to study languages at the university, with the hope of pursuing a career within the finance industry. I was selected as a candidate for the three-day insight programmes at Bank of America Merrill Lynch, JPMorgan, and Morgan Stanley. During these programmes, it was emphasised that it does not necessarily matter what you study at university as long as you do well and achieve at least a 2:1. They welcome applications from students with humanities backgrounds as they work differently to people with more technical backgrounds. This reassured me that I could still study the subjects I really enjoyed and that it would not hinder me from pursuing my chosen career.

Prior to moving into sixth form, I had made the decision to make an application to Cambridge University. This is because I knew that I had the potential to make it there and that it was one of the best universities for my chosen degree (German and Latin). In year 12, I worked diligently in all my subjects. I read ahead and outside of the syllabus and visited museums, exhibitions, etc. in order to give myself the best preparation for any potential interview. In the summer before year 13, I drafted my personal statement (which I redrafted countless times before I was satisfied!) and visited Cambridge for a weeklong summer school, which I was successful in gaining a place at. I received five As at AS level and had an average UMS score of 94/100. This gave me confidence as I knew that Cambridge usually called applicants who had an average UMS score of 85+ to interview. When I was in year 13, I had to submit two essays (one in German and another based on a Latin text) and a supplementary personal statement explaining why I particularly wanted to go to Cambridge and do this specific course. I was successful in being called for an interview at Trinity College, which took place in December 2013. I had to sit an exam, and I had two interviews—one for German and one for Latin, both of which I was given texts to prepare before I went in for discussion. The interviews were engaging and interesting, and I truly did enjoy myself despite being nervous. On my eighteenth birthday in January 2014, I received confirmation that I had gained admission to Trinity College on a conditional offer of achieving A*AA in my A levels, with the A* being in either German or Latin. The stipulation of the A* was typical of the college I applied to, whereas most other colleges ask for A*AA with the A* in any subject.

This was a proud moment for my family and me because I had worked so hard in my education and my parents had been so supportive of me. I continued to work hard in year 13 and began revision early in order to ensure that I knew my syllabus inside out. My teachers had given me a prediction of three A*s (German, Latin, and economics), which I had considered quite scary as it meant I was under pressure to achieve quite highly, but I used that fear to motivate me to work even harder. My exams were challenging, but I managed to get through them by the grace of God. In August 2014, I received my A-level results, and I achieved A*AA; however, the A* was in economics, and the As were in German and Latin. Consequently, this meant that I had narrowly missed my offer from Trinity College, Cambridge. However, the admissions office notified me that they had placed me in the summer pool, a selection of candidates whom they highly recommend for other colleges to pick from if they have remaining spaces. Unfortunately, after a few days of deliberation, Trinity informed me that the other colleges did not have any remaining spaces and were unable to make me an unconditional offer.

Thus, I was firmly accepted by my insurance choice, UCL (University College London), where I began my degree in September 2014. Upon joining UCL, I was able to pick all my modules for first year from both the German and Latin side of my degree, which is unique to the degree at UCL because at other universities, some (if not all) modules in first year are compulsory. This meant that I was studying things I had a strong interest in and was exploring areas that I had never studied before but by choice. My departments were set up in a way that there were no lectures, but I attended classes which focused on discussion of material prepared beforehand. My classes were also very small, ranging from eight to twenty people. This allows for a more intimate environment where questions may be asked and answered in full, in comparison to other degrees where there are lecture halls with 400 students and one lecturer speaking at them for an hour. I had regular weekly assignments from most classes, which I received feedback from. During the year, I had to complete multiple essays and research projects, the most interesting of which being a research project I conducted on the African diaspora in Europe and whether its increased presence in the recent decades has produced a new racism. The fact that I was able to undertake such research under a module called 'Black Europe' is a testament to the fact that I am able to choose from such a wide and varied selection of modules and that I am also able to independently pursue my own interests within those modules.

Aside from academics, I have also immersed myself into the university experience by getting involved in extracurricular activities. I joined societies like Women in Finance, Economics and Finance, African and Caribbean, and many more. These societies had been a great way for me to make friends, expand my network, gain new skills, and broaden my skill set. In addition to this, I was heavily involved in the academic student staff committees for my department (German) and the School of European Languages and Culture, which my department came under. This year (2015), I had the role of the first year representative on both committees, where I represented the views of over 400 students, and I was also a StAR (student academic representative). Doing this allowed me to get to know senior members of staff within the university, which had been helpful in changing aspects of the system which other students might have issues with. I also took steps towards pursuing my chosen career path within investment banking. I completed a weeklong internship known as a Spring Week in April 2015 at RBS, the investment bank within Corporate and Institutional Banking, which I achieved after being fast-tracked to interview from an A-level insight programme I completed in August 2014. After the Spring Week, I was contacted and told that, as a result of my performance during the week, I was fast-tracked to an interview for the ten-week summer internship in 2016 (for which the application process does not usually begin until September). I had the interview in June, and at the time of writing this, I am awaiting the result.

Overall, I have enjoyed my first year of university because I feel like I have been involved in quite a lot of various activities, both academic and extracurricular, which have improved my transferable skills and developed me as a person. I learned a lot about myself and have learned to be more resilient and proactive. I know that the foundation that my parents, Mr Gilbert Gbedawo, and my primary and secondary schools have given me has enabled me to support myself academically, mentally, emotionally, and financially while at the university. I am looking forward to the rest of my university experience, particularly my year abroad in my third year (September 2016–July 2017), which I will spend in Germany, either studying at university or working or both! I am also confident that by God's grace I shall finish university well, graduating with a first-class or upper second-class honours degree.

Vanessa, like many other students who have achieved outstanding results in external examinations and in their studies worked hard. They persevered through challenging times, and they asked for help and support when they needed to. But most importantly, they work with their parents and teachers to achieve their personal educational goals.

It is my hope that their stories will motivate and encourage all of us to become active players in the journey towards educational excellence. When we all play our part with excellence, diligence, and determination, then success is inevitable.

CHAPTER 8

How to Maximise Learning

Once, I was teaching in an outstanding inner London school, and I observed that on the walls of the classroom were posters about the various types of learners. I thought to myself, this is amazing. This piece of knowledge is worth sharing with every student and must be repeatedly emphasised till it becomes the guiding principles which will make every learner an outstanding student just as this very school is, and I hope it will remain an outstanding school.

Responsible Learners

- These students know right from wrong and make good choices: They know when to play and when to study. They know when to listen and when to talk. They know when to use mobile phones and when not to. They know and understand the difference in every season, and so they maximise every opportunity.

- They are capable of managing themselves: These students manage their learning and resources very well. They have the right tools of learning and are capable of managing these tools. They can work independently and as part of a group without distracting others. They do not blame others for their situation but are eager to take responsibility.

- They help other students and are willing to receive help and support when they also need it.

- They think ahead: Thinking is crucial for success. It is quite different from daydreaming. Thinkers find solutions to problems by devising different ways of resolving a problem. These students think ahead. They think about the curriculum, the topics they need to master, and the areas of difficulty. They think about the questions they will ask, the books they will need, how to organise their studies and timetables, and even how to study well and prepare in advance for their examinations.

Resourceful Learners

A resourceful person is one that is ingenious, capable, and full of initiative. These students take initiative for learning and are capable of undertaking personal learning. They exhibit the following traits:

- They show initiative: These students take action regarding learning without being prompted by a teacher or coerced by parents. They know that learning will increase success, so they are happy to learn, and they do it.

- They can learn, and they use different methods of learning: In learning, these students vary the methods and approach they use. They know when it is best to use laptops and computers or when to go to the library. They know when to learn with peers and have discussions or when to study on their own. They also know when to ask for support from their teachers or whether to ask parents to invest in a tutor on a one-to-one basis. They know what they want and are able to communicate that effectively.

- They ask questions and are flexible in their approach towards learning: Questions introduce you to answers. It is vital that every teaching and learning transaction be underpinned by questions. This will help the learner to understand the concepts taught and consolidate the outcomes of the learning. The learner must and should always have a question book so that any question that comes up during learning can be documented and then asked at any given opportunity.

The Reflective Learners

- They are curious: These students are never satisfied with the status quo, and they ask why things are the way that they are and try to find answers to the big questions. It is said that many people saw the apple fall, but Isaac Newton asked *why* and then discovered that gravity pulls object to the centre of the earth.

- They can describe their progress and set targets for the future: Every learner should have a clear understanding of where they are in their learning journey. They must know their areas of strength as well as areas that need improvement so that they can set realistic and achievable target to reach through learning and, if needed, get the extra support needed to reach those targets.

- They listen to and learn from feedback: Feedback is important if you are going to improve on your current performance. Great athletes who excel in their sports have coaches that give them feedback and correct them. I love the game of tennis, and currently, the world number one is Djokovic. He surrounds himself with a team of former champions, and it is not surprising he is the world number one. Another example is the great champion Serena William. Ever since taking on a new coach, she has been explosive and currently is the world number one as far as women tennis is concerned. They listen and take feedback, and sometimes while they appear to be losing a set in a game, they look up to where their respective coaches are for feedback.

STEPS TOWARDS EDUCATIONAL EXCELLENCE

Likewise, any student who is going to rise to become a distinguished learner and achiever must learn to take feedback and make the necessary corrections to excel.

- They learn from experience: These students understand the importance of every teaching and learning experience that they have at school or with their teachers, parents, or carers. They learn from those experiences and use them as a launch pad for greater success.

The Resilient Learner

- They persist with their learning: These students do not give up when the going gets tough; rather, they persevere till they overcome the initial challenge or setback. They reach out for help and support till they master the areas of difficulty.

- They have a positive attitude: These students have a winning attitude towards their teachers, school, peers, classmates, staff, and parents. The thing about attitude is that it can draw people to you or put people off. I have heard it said again and again that your attitude in life determines your altitude—your position or placement. Uncommon students and learners have a positive attitude. They are thankful and grateful always. They show respect and honour to both parents and teachers alike. They carry themselves with dignity and are very considerate and selfless.

- I am privileged to teach students from all backgrounds: I am always drawn to those with positive attitude. I want to explain more, teach them some more, and pour myself into them. I want them to succeed, and I want to mentor and help them. I want to give them the resources that I have and to recommend books and resources that will benefit them. Such is the power of a positive attitude.

John Maxwell defines an attitude as an inward feeling expressed by behaviour. It is important to nurture the seeds that will make you exhibit the right and winning attitude towards life and your studies.

What is your attitude towards your parents, your siblings, your family, your teachers, and your mentors? Remember that if you are grateful and thankful, you will attract good people, and with that comes support, help, encouragement, and every good thing you can imagine.

If you sow the seeds of disrespect and ungratefulness, you will repel good people from you, and you are likely going to attract negative people to you. My wish is that you will be wise enough to be selective with whom you associate with and be able to maintain positive relationships.

- They stay involve with learning and take personal responsibility for it: Learning is a key requirement for personal growth and development. That is why nations invest substantially in education and schools so that they can develop the human capital necessary for the economic and social development of their nations.

It has been demonstrated time and again that there is a positive correlation between quality education and socio-economic development of nations. If you are going to succeed in your studies, then you must stay involve with your learning. It is not the responsibility of your teachers alone to impart knowledge; you must be ready and be prepared to receive and seek after knowledge. Start today to develop an action plan for your learning, and stick to your plan. The rest will be success and higher achievement.

As I write to you this section of the book, it is my thirty-eighth birthday. As I look back, I am grateful to God for His protection and blessings upon my life and my family. I remember how, as a child growing up, we used to walk miles to get to school from the nation of Ghana to Togo just to access quality education at that time. I am grateful to my aunties, uncles, teachers, and especially my godfather Mr Anthony Avornyo, who believed in education so much that he would get an extra tutor to teach us after school at home when we were in primary school and this tradition was later repeated by my dad during my holidays with him and the rest of the family in Abeokuta in Nigeria.

I recall in my youth when I spent the holidays with my dad and my siblings in Abeokuta, Nigeria. My dad would register me for extra coaching and lesson in some of the top grammar schools in Abeokuta, Nigeria. Looking back, I am grateful to my parents and guardians for investing in my education. I am thankful for the books and the opportunities given to me by my stepmother, Elizabeth. She bought a suitcase of books and clothes and boxes of provisions when I was about to go to a boarding school for my secondary education and continued this during my secondary education. I cannot tell you enough about the support and care of my three wonderful aunties Rose, Christiana, and Josephine. May the Lord bless you all for the investments you made in my life. I am here today because you allowed God to use you all to raise me up when my mum suddenly passed on to eternity in a fatal car accident, which I survived by the hand of God. May her soul rest in perfect and absolute peace.

What will I say about my teachers? They are an absolute delight. They nurtured and believed in me and taught me well. God bless them all.

I also took the responsibility and stayed involved with my learning and still do. The Lord has since taken me from one level of goodness to another. Praise the Lord forever!

My wish for you reading this book is that you will receive inspiration and rise above the challenges confronting your learning and development and that God will raise help for you. I hope that the people who will help and support your

GILBERT GBEDAWO

learning and development will step into your life from now and that your attitude will attract the right people. I also pray that your dreams of educational excellence and a successful life for you and your family become a reality.

- They set targets and practise: Practice makes perfect. I love sports, especially athletics and tennis. I admire winners, record holders, and record-breakers. The key to breaking records lies in the many hours these great achievers spend practising and rehearsing for a tournament or an event. They do it on their own, with support of their families or coaches ahead of the event itself. Sometimes these people do it when it is favourable and convenient, but most times, they do it when it is unfavourable and cold. They wake up early to practise. They work hard and even harder in anticipation of the moment of glory. They set targets and goals. They put in the hours and then more hours. Sometimes they win, and sometimes they don't, yet they never give up. They never quit. They stay in the competition till the day of their breakthrough, and soon after that, they go back to train and keep training for another tournament or event. They have mental strength and fortitude. They know that the best is yet to come, so they keep going till they win.

If you are going to become excellent and attain uncommon success, you must set targets and get busy working on your targets. It is possible to move from average to outstanding. It is doable, so just start today and do it! When you do it daily, weekly, monthly, and yearly, then and only then will you become a celebrity in your field of study and, later on, in life. God bless you as you set target. Work and practise daily because in the words of Dr Mike Murdock, 'Successful people do daily what unsuccessful people do occasionally'.

CHAPTER 9

Charity Begins at Home: Role of Parents

Teach them to your children, talking about them when you sit at home and when you walk along the road, when you lie down and when you get up. (Deuteronomy 11:19)

Train up a child in the way he should go: and when he is old he will not depart from it. (Proverbs 22:6)

These things command and teach. Let no man despise thy youth; but be thou an example of the believers, in word, in conversation, in charity, in spirit, in faith, in purity. Till I come, give attendance to reading, to exhortation, to doctrine. (1 Timothy 5:11–13)

Thank you for investing your time to read this chapter. It is my prayer that it will bless you and help you to take the steps to maximise your role as a parent and equip you with the knowledge to raise outstanding children who will shine the light of Christ to a world ready and eager for the manifestation of the sons of God. I pray that your home will be a place where the next generation of leaders will be raised. I pray that great things will be birthed in you through the reading of this chapter and, indeed, your home will be filled with the love and the peace of God that transcends knowledge.

The word 'charity' means 'giving help, money, food to those in need', but it also denotes a kindly and lenient attitude towards people. It further means, simply put, 'love for fellow human beings', so we can say love begins at home.

As you read this book, there are a lot of homes where love is lacking. A lot of homes are experiencing hatred, strife, tension, suffering, rejection, violence, neglect, abuse, and all forms of injustice, but at the same time, there are homes today that are filled with peace, love, acceptance, and warmth.

The home is crucial to the well-being of a child because it is the place where the first teachings and nurturing begins. The home is fundamental to the total and holistic development of children because it is the place where children are prepared to fit into their communities.

The home can position children to reach out and become strong, loving, caring, positive leaders of tomorrow, or the home can paralyse and derail the aspirations, goals, dreams, and ultimately, the future well-being of children and sometime adults alike.

I have always wondered how some families are able to produce generations of leaders, presidents, CEOs of companies, wealthy business owners, entrepreneurs, pastors, bishops, teachers, architects, medical doctors, scientists, members of parliaments, and outstanding politicians while some families merely reproduce children that end up with all kinds of vices. Some of these children struggle in life and are full of hate. They join gangs and indulge in tendencies that derail their future hopes.

When you trace these negative outcomes later in life, you will discover that sometimes the seeds of failure were sown during their childhood, and later on in life, we see or witness the effects and the ramifications of poor upbringing.

I pray that your home will be a place where champions and leaders are raised. Sometimes the challenges of parenting can be daunting, but when you rely on the wisdom of God, then and only

STEPS TOWARDS EDUCATIONAL EXCELLENCE

then can you be empowered to live up to your role as a parent because by strength shall no man prevail. We all need the help of God and the support of good role models to be able to discharge the responsibility of parenthood.

A loving home is necessary and fundamental to the success of children in school and later on in life as a child is not just the product of the genes inherited from the parents but, most importantly, the product of how, why, where, and who raised them and nurtured them.

This initial socialisation and training begin at home. It is an opportunity that must be taken seriously because you never know that the child you are raising today may end up becoming the next prime minister, like Joseph in Egypt, President Barack Obama of the USA, or the Prime Minister, David Cameron of the United Kingdom.

The child you are raising today may become the next big phenomenon that may happen to the world, so do not despise the days of little beginnings. It is fascinating to watch Lewis Hamilton, the double world champion of Formula 1 racing or the tennis played by Serena Williams or Roger Federer or Rafael Nadal or the British number one Andy Murray. I always thank God for the parents and the team who, against all odds, stand to nurture the seeds of greatness that now bring joy and happiness to millions around the world through their success stories and achievements. Other parents have overcome challenging economic and social circumstances to raise outstanding men and women who we all admire and all these people are examples to us of what can be achieved through determination, hard work, and perseverance.

Look at the parents of Moses and Jesus Christ, who, despite the harsh political climates of their time where male children were being slaughtered by insecure governmental regime, withstood the threats of death and danger to raise a prophet for the Israelites and a saviour of the world. These parents were motivated by unconditional and unfeigned love to raise the next generation against all odds. This love is rooted in taking responsibility as

GILBERT GBEDAWO

parents and not delegating it to others who may play supportive role rather than the primary role. I pray for you to rise to this responsibility and receive grace to function as a parent or a foster parent.

Do you realise that the state of your home later determines the landscape of your community and, ultimately, the nation? Hence, it is vital that the children you are privileged of raising at home, are well looked after, taught, supported, trained, mentored, encouraged, and positively planned for. In other words, great investment must be made into the spiritual enrichment, educational provision, material, healthcare, and social empowerment, and that is my motivation to write this book.

The love of your children should always motivate you to go the extra mile to teach them when they are young rather than delegate the duty of care entirely to others. It must start with you in the privacy of your home, where you are the first role model and teacher.

I would like you to take a moment to reflect on the childhood you have had. Think about all the people who made it memorable, meaningful, and successful. What words did they use, and how did they show love and affection? How did they express their care, and how did they demonstrate care for you? I have fond memories of my childhood, and I am grateful for the people the Lord used to nurture and raise me up. Sometimes the conditions were challenging, but when I look back, I am thankful and grateful to God and to the support, love, discipline, and care I received.

In life, all things work together for the good of those who love the Lord and are called according to His purpose, so let me encourage you to look back and be grateful for your childhood, whether it was pleasant or difficult, because sometimes greatness is born in the womb of adversity.

Why don't you go a step further and give these people a call if they are still alive to express your gratitude and show your honour? Buy a gift to express and sow a seed of honour and gratitude to them for being there for you in times of vulnerability and tenderness. Show honour for their patience, endurance, and tenacity. They deserve to be appreciated and celebrated.

Now it is your turn to love and be kind to your own children or the children you have adopted. It is now your time to demonstrate and empower the next generation.

Maybe your childhood was not as pleasant as you may have wished. It could be that your childhood was filled with neglect, rejection, abuse, or difficulty. Now that you are in a position to do better, arise and take up your place so that the next generation may exceed you and excel in life.

Irrespective of how challenging your own experiences might have been, remember that you are not able to turn back the hands of time, but instead, you can choose how you will respond to the future.

Where you have known sorrow and pain, I pray that you will have joy and happiness. I pray that the attitude of thanksgiving will nullify every regret and complaint. It is worth knowing that sometimes great men and women were born or raised in the midst of severe hardship and difficulty; however, they rose above the challenges and are now shining and in charge.

Now that you are a parent, receive the grace to assume your place of responsibility and change your paradigm and mindset so you can create a brighter future for your children.

> When I was a child, I talked like a child, I reasoned like a child. When I became a man I put the ways of childhood behind me. (1 Corinthians 13:11)

The above scriptural reference suggests that there is a way children talk, think, process information, reason, or behave. It further indicates that adults or parents should depart from childhood tendencies or dispositions and assume the responsibility of adulthood. This positions parents to be able to fully discharge their responsibility of raising and leading their children effectively.

A child's world revolves around their parents and the adults in the immediate environment. A child depends on parents for virtually everything—food, clothing, shelter, and tender loving care. Children talk, think, and reason in a particular way because they do not understand and are oblivious to the bigger picture. They are not concerned by the implications of external factors or prevailing circumstance. They are dependent on the judgement and support of their parents.

It would be catastrophic or disastrous if the parents refuse to assume responsibility by also talking and behaving like a child and reasoning like a child. If this happens, it's likely that the family unit will fail rather than succeed. This is also likely to have negative consequences on the community where this family is located. I pray for you to *rise* up and *be* who you are meant to be in the life of your children.

I pray that you receive grace and find strength to build your home with patience, wisdom, and knowledge.

> The wise woman builds her house, but with her own hands the foolish one tears hers down. (Proverbs 14:1)

We are encouraged to build our homes (with wisdom). Those who build homes are wise because the home is the foundation of every society or a nation. The stronger the homes, the better and more prosperous the nation.

Therefore, be encouraged to rise up and build your home today with love because charity begins at home.

Every building requires serious planning. It is therefore prudent and wise to first and foremost carry out a comprehensive overview and analysis of where your home currently is.

Be genuine and honest to yourselves. Carry out a SWOT analysis of your home.

1. Identify the strengths: These may include a loving and supportive spouse, a source of regular income, being part

of a loving and caring church where the Word of God is taught, supportive love circle consisting of parents, in-laws, mentors, etc.

2. Identify the weaknesses: these are situations that are contrary to your physical, emotional, financial and mental well-being.

3. Name your opportunities: Count all your blessings, testimonies, and victories. Prospect and make the most out of all the opportunities you currently have, especially the opportunity to be a parent, whether as a dad or a mum.

4. Identify the threats or fears: list all of your fears and find effective ways to face those fears.

After you have carried out the SWOT analysis, it is vital to invest quality time to plan a strategy to overcome and triumph over the current challenges, bearing in mind that all things are subject to change their state of being when the appropriate force is applied, so now, go into *action* and apply the force of *prayer*, wise action, and work.

> For which of you intending to build a tower, does not sit down first and count the cost, whether he has enough to finish it, lest, after he has laid the foundation, and is not able to finish, all who see it begin to mock him, saying, this man began to build and was not able to finish? (Luke 14:28–30)

The first principle towards any worthwhile project is to *sit down*. This posture is absolutely necessary before the start of building your home, your children, their future, their education, their development.

Sitting down allows you to take inventory of all available resources at your disposal. When you sit down, you can recall better, you can reflect better, you can think better, you can reason better. You are more likely to relax and consider and analyse more carefully. It is therefore necessary to *sit down* before you start to count the *cost*.

GILBERT GBEDAWO

Our schools, universities, banks, and other major institutions are filled with chairs and tables to allow students, bankers, and politicians to sit down. Possibly as you read this book, you are sitting in a comfortable sofa or on a chair. I write this for you while sitting in my office chair.

Do you always sit down first before initiating projects? Be encouraged to sit down first to ensure you consider almost every aspect of the next major project you intend to embark on. This may be sending your children to very good schools or private education. It may be opening or starting an investment portfolio for your children or building a family dream home. Sit down before you count the cost.

Do you have enough resources to *start* and *finish* what you are building? Be realistic with yourself. Are you a good finisher? Did you complete your last project or assignment, or is it work in progress? Did you abandon the last project? Whatever your answer is, I pray that you receive the finisher's *grace* to complete that which you start in Jesus' precious name.

> I have fought the good fight. I have finished the race. I have kept the faith or I have remained faithful. (2 Timothy 4:7)
>
> And I am certain that God, who began the good work within you, will continue his work until it is finally finished on the day Christ Jesus returns. (Philippians 1:6)

Precious reader and parent, I pray for you today that every project you are about to launch with the objective of building your family and home shall receive the grace and blessing of God. I pray that you will excel and finish that project in Jesus' precious name. It is the desire of our heavenly Father, who is the author and finisher of our faith, that we complete everything we have started.

It gives God pleasure when you are doing well and living the abundant life He has promised in His Word. That good work you have started to ensure the well-being of your household shall be perfected in Jesus' name. Irrespective of your immediate circumstances, you will overcome if you believe and hold fast the confession of your faith.

Let me assure you by the Word of God that your home from today will experience the love, joy, and blessings of God because your heavenly Father promised that when John wrote:

> Behold, I wish above all things that you may prosper and
> be in health, even as your soul prospers. (3 John 1:2)

The plan and purpose of God for every home and family who recognises and acknowledges His Son Jesus Christ as the Lord and Saviour is prosperity, peace, and good health.

That is why Jesus was born, crucified, and rose again. Jesus had to complete his assignment to demonstrate the love of God by dying on the cross at Calvary. He paid the full price for the redemption of every member of your family so that the peace of God that surpasses all understanding may dwell richly in you.

> When he had received the drink, Jesus said, 'It is finished'.
> With that He bowed his head and gave up his spirit. (John
> 19:30)

> Behold, what manner of love the Father has bestowed on
> us, that we should be called sons of God! Therefore the
> world does not know us, because it did not know Him. (1
> John 3)

Beloved reader, to experience the greatest and purest form of love in your family and home, it is vital to acknowledge Jesus as your saviour who lived to die so that we can be born into the family of God, and if you are already a member of his family and the church, then you are qualified by the blood of Jesus to experience divine love and receive grace to build a home that glorifies God and honours Him.

However, if you doubt or not sure of your salvation, then pray this prayer, and today you can become part of God's family, and in this way, you can also build with love.

> Heavenly Father, I thank You for sending Your Son, Jesus Christ to die for my sins so that I can become part of your family here on earth. I confess this day that Jesus is the son of God who died for my sins. I receive Jesus into my life today.
>
> I acknowledge my sins and shortcomings, and I ask for your forgiveness in the name of Jesus Christ, who is now my Lord and Saviour.
>
> Thank you for accepting me into your beloved family in Jesus' name. Amen.

Congratulations, precious and beloved member of the family of God. Now receive the grace and wisdom to become a great parent or a son or a daughter and build your own family, home, dreams, and desires with love.

May the love of God fill your heart and mind. I pray that God's Word will dwell in your heart richly and the wisdom of God, which is the Bible, the Word of God, will make you a great builder of lives in Jesus' precious name. Now go further by becoming a member of a local church in your city or town to grow in wisdom and knowledge.

The psalmist tells us in Psalm 127:3–5:

> Behold, children are a gift of the Lord, the fruit of the womb is a reward. Like arrows in the hand of a warrior, so are the children of one's youth.
>
> How blessed is the man whose quiver is full of them. They will not be ashamed when they speak with their enemies in the gate.

STEPS TOWARDS EDUCATIONAL EXCELLENCE

From the above scripture, it is worth remembering that your children are gifts of the Lord, and if you are pregnant now with a child, remember that this is a reward, so just thank God for His goodness and mercy towards you.

Our heavenly Father is a good God. He is the giver of all good and precious gifts. He gave us eyes to see, mouth to speak, hands to reach and hold, and the very air that we breathe. Stop now and thank God.

> The LORD visited Sarah as He had said and the Lord did for her as He had promised. For Sarah became pregnant and bore Abraham a son in his old age, at the set time God had told him.
>
> And Sarah said God has made me to laugh; all who hear will laugh with me. (Genesis 21:1–2, 6)

My precious friend, when you thank and bless God for who He is and how far He has brought you, then you qualify to receive even more. I pray for your home and family to receive the visitation of the Lord.

I also pray for you now that you will laugh again after all that you have been through—the trials, the valleys, the battles, and the silent storm. I pray for the joy of God to envelop your heart. Remember, your best days are ahead. Like Sarah, you will laugh again, and those who will hear your triumph over adversity will laugh with you.

Do not give up! Do not give in! Precious reader, there is light at the end of the tunnel, but I pray for your home even now to receive light as you go through the tunnels and valleys of the shadow of death. Just say aloud, 'The Lord is my light and my salvation so whom shall I fear' (Psalm 27:1).

Beloved, sometimes we all confront situations that may be overwhelming. Maybe you have done everything you need to do to build a home of love, and yet your spouse does not appreciate your effort or the children do not seem to appreciate your investment of time and energy. Please do not throw in the towel because a change is around the corner. It could be that the bills are too much to pay or the doctors have given a bad medical report or you have come to the end of the road and you think your back is against the wall.

Are you facing persecution and attack from those who should love and protect you? Like David in Psalm 3:1–3, you may be asking, 'Lord, how are they increased that trouble me? Many are they that rise up against me. Many there be which say of my soul there is no help for him in God.'

Wait a minute. Look at verse 3 and just declare: 'But thou, O Lord, art a shield for me; my glory and the lifter up of mine head.'

What you are going through right now will not destroy you but will position you to see the helps of God and goodness of Jehovah. Consider this beautiful testimony of Hagar, who faced eviction from the household of Abraham after her son mocked his half-brother Isaac. Hagar lost favour in the sight of her mistress Sarah and so was asked to leave the comfort and familiarity of the only place she knew as home.

She found herself confronted with the harshness of uncharted territory. She was isolated and on her own without help. Her only supplies of food and water ran out. Her son was hungry and thirsty. There was no source of food or water. They were faced with the wilderness experience, and there was nowhere and nobody to turn to for assistance.

Sometimes life may throw all sorts of things at you and your family without warning.

Maybe your teenage son or daughter is causing so much pain right now and you do not know what to do. It may be that you know a friend or a loved one who is going through difficulty to raise a family.

I pray for you right now that, just as Hagar and her family experienced divine intervention in the wilderness season of their lives, you also will receive divine intervention.

Now consider the account in Genesis 21:14–20:

> So Abraham rose early in the morning and took bread and a bottle of water and gave them to Hagar, putting them on her shoulders and he sent her and the youth away. And she wandered on and lost her way in the wilderness of Beersheba.
>
> When the water in the bottle was all gone, Hagar caused the youth to lie down under one of the shrubs.
>
> Then she went and sat down opposite him a good way off about a bowshot for she said, Let me not see the death of the lad. And as she sat down opposite him, he lifted up his voice and wept and she raised her voice and wept.
>
> And God heard the voice of the youth and the angel of God called to Hagar out of heaven and said to her, 'What troubles you, Hagar? Fear not, for God has heard the voice of the youth where he is? Arise, raise up the youth and support him with your hand, for I intend to make him a great nation.'
>
> Then God opened her eyes and she saw a well of water; and she went and filled the empty bottle with water and caused the youth to drink.
>
> And God was with the youth and he dwelt in the wilderness and became an archer.

Just this morning as I was getting ready to continue writing, I heard a knock on the door. I opened the door, and behold, it was Pastor Smart and his wife. The couple brought to me and my family a box of De Vina red grape drinks, toiletries, and twenty kilograms of rice among other things. We are thankful for these gifts and for the blessings of God.

May the Lord bless them and increase them more and more.

I pray for you now that people will rise to show you kindness and favour as God touches their hearts to bless you in Jesus' name.

Now let us consider carefully the response and the approach of Hagar when she was confronted with the challenge of raising her son as a single parent.

Obviously, it was clear that Hagar ran out of ideas and resources, so she decided to distance herself from the problem. She put her son somewhere and went a good way off. Usually when there is a problem in a family or home, some parents refuse to acknowledge that there is a problem. They choose to bury their heads in the sand like the proverbial ostrich. Some play the blame game and refuse to take responsibility. Some pretend there is no problem. Some choose to walk away from the challenge altogether.

Interestingly, the youth cried out for help and relief. I love the approach of the young child. This compelled the mother to also raise her voice and weep.

God responded to the desperation of the young child by allowing the angel to visit Hagar and provide a solution to the crisis. However, the most important part of the conversation was not just the provision of water to quench the thirst of Ishmael but also the prophetic declaration that God issued to the mother concerning the destiny and the future of Ishmael, who was helpless and desperate to survive.

> Arise, raise up the youth and support him with your hand
> for I intend to make him a great nation. (Genesis 21:18)

It is my firm belief that God is still declaring these prophetic words, especially to every single parent who is struggling to raise their children or sacrificing everything to provide them the best shelter, accommodation, food, clothing, and most importantly, education and training.

This is the time to arise and raise your son or daughter. It is the time to support your child with your hands because, like Ishmael, God intends to make your son or daughter a great nation—a source of blessing to the world.

There is greatness in your child; therefore, your hands must not be weak. There are gifts and talents that are now lying dormant in your child, but you must take responsibility to support that child and nurture the seeds of greatness in them. This is no time to complain, cry, or give up. It is time to arise and do something for that child.

The child may look small right now, but sooner or later, you will realise that every great thing starts small. Bishop T. D. Jakes once preached a sermon entitled 'Great Things Come in Small Packages'. It is therefore not surprising that we are admonished in the scripture not to take for granted the days of small beginnings.

> Though your beginning was small, yet thy latter end should greatly increase. (Job 8:7)

Your family may look or feel insignificant in your sight, but be assured that with the right support and care, it will blossom and become great. I am always encouraged by the life and testimony of our senior pastor Mathew Ashimolowo of the Kingsway International Christian Centre in Buckmore Park, Chatham, who, against all odds and challenges during his childhood, is now an example to millions around the world. His life and ministry are a testament that with God all things are possible. He is my hero and inspiration. He teaches us to break every invisible barrier of limitation and to cross the lines meant to stop us from becoming champions. One of my favourites of his quotes and declarations is 'I am a barrier breaker! I am a line crosser!'

What makes the difference is the willingness and the ability to remain focused and determined to nurture, monitor, and keep

Building to Last

> Unless the LORD builds the house, its builders labour uselessly. Unless the LORD guards the city, its security forces keep watch uselessly. (Psalm 127:1)

> By wisdom a house is built, and by understanding it is established. (Proverbs 24:3)

Every building, including your home, will someday be tested by the forces of nature or some form of contrary wind. However, the foundation set out at the beginning shall determine if the building or your home is capable of remaining after the stormy weather or turbulence. Some homes crack while others are completely destroyed by the storms of life. Yet others flourish and get stronger by using the wind to soar higher like the eagle to greater heights.

I pray for you today that the storms of life will only take you to greater heights and testimonies. You are not for destruction, but instead, you will outlast the storm.

There are different forms of storms, but the purpose is always the same. Sometimes storms may arise as a result of ignoring or disobeying the Word of the Lord or unfaithfulness by a member of a family, or it may arise due to health issues or financial crisis or a sudden loss of a spouse or a loved one. Sometimes it may be a life-threatening experience, such as a tragic accident or loss of job. Whatever form it may take, the intention is to cause havoc and leave behind a trail of destruction and chaos, but with God, you will prevail.

> For he commanded and raised the stormy wind which lifted up the waves thereof. They mount up to the heavens. The go down again to the depths: their soul is melted because of trouble.

> The reel to and fro, and stagger like a drunken man, and are at their wits end then they cry unto the Lord in their trouble, and he brought them out of their distresses.
>
> He maketh the storm a calm, so that the waves thereof are still. Then are they glad because they be quiet so he brought them unto their desired haven. (Psalm 107:25–30)

Precious friend, the actual intention of every storm is to prevent you from getting to your desired haven. The desired haven could be your dream, aspiration, desired purpose, a blessed family, a successful business, a progressive career, good relationships, social networks, health and well-being, or a prosperous life and ministry. Storms also have the capacity to trouble your soul and cause emotional turbulence. It may cause you to have a sense of loss momentarily. But you will recover, and you will get there.

The song writer posed a question when he wrote:

> Will your anchor hold in the storms of life, when the clouds unfold their wings of strife? When the strong tides lift and the cables strain, will your anchor drift, or firm remain?

In other words, would you still praise and thank God even though you have not yet reached your desired haven? Would you still say that God is good even though you are yet to see the tangibility of His promise? Would you still hold unto vows you have exchanged during your wedding or holy matrimony in spite of the disagreement with your spouse? Would you still love her or him despite the contrary wind that blows across the serenity of your residence? Would you still hold unto the Word of God despite the negative and bad report? Would you still remain in faith and trust when it seems as though all hope is gone?

I love the response of the songwriter. It goes like this:

> We have an anchor that keeps the soul. Steadfast and sure while the billows roll, fastened to the ROCK which cannot move, grounded firm and deep in the Saviour's love.

If your life, home and family is going to outlast the storms of life, then it must have Jesus Christ as the FOUNDATION.

Hebrews 6:19–20 notes:

> Which hope we have as an anchor of the soul, both sure and steadfast and which entirety into that within the veil. Whither the forerunner is for us entered even Jesus, made a high priest forever after the order of Melchisedec.

Now that you are building on the foundation who is the Lord Jesus Christ, I can assure you that your home and family would last the test of time. However, there are decisions that you must make so that the home is filled with peace, joy, and love.

These decisions will further strengthen you and make your children stronger, more prosperous, and sound to succeed academically, spiritually, and socially. They will become leaders and champions in due course.

Seven Decisions That Will Decide a Stronger Home

1. Your Decision to Stay in the Word of God

> Teach them to your children, talking about them when you sit at home and when you walk along the road, when you lie down and when you get up. (Deuteronomy 11:19)

> If you fully obey the LORD your God and carefully follow all his commands I give you today, the LORD your God will set you high above all the nations on earth. (Deuteronomy 28:1)

> My son, listen to your father's instruction, and do not let go of your mother's teaching. (Proverbs 1:8)

> This book of the law shall not depart out of thy mouth; but thou shalt meditate therein day and night, that thou

mayest observe to do according to all that is written therein: for then thou shalt make thy way prosperous, and then thou shalt have good success. (Joshua 1:8)

Let the wise hear and increase in learning, and the one who understands obtain guidance. (Proverbs 1:5)

But don't just listen to God's word. You must do what it says. Otherwise, you are only fooling yourselves. (James 1:22)

Only take heed to thyself and keep thy soul diligently, lest thou forget the things which thine eyes have seen and lest they depart from thy heart all the days of thy life: but teach them thy sons and thy sons' sons . . . and I will make them hear my words that they may learn to fear me all the days that they shall live upon the earth, and that they may teach their children. (Deuteronomy 4:9–10)

And the Lord commanded me at that time to teach you statutes and judgements that ye might do them in the land whither ye go over to possess it. (Deuteronomy 4:14)

Let the word of Christ dwell in you richly in all wisdom; teaching and admonishing one another in psalms and hymns and spiritual songs, singing with grace in your heart to the Lord. (Colossians 3:22)

Praise ye the Lord, Blessed is the man that feareth the Lord, that delighted greatly in his commandments.

His seed shall be mighty upon earth. The generation of the upright shall be blessed. Wealth and riches shall be in his house and his righteousness endureth forever. (Psalm 112:1–3)

Teach me good judgement and knowledge: for I have believed thy commandments. Before I was afflicted I went astray: but now have I kept thy word.

> Thou are good and doest good; teach me thy statutes.
>
> The law of thy mouth is better unto me than thousands of gold and silver. (Psalm 119:66–68, 72)

The decision to teach your children the Word of God will cause them to be wise and shrewd because the Word of God is the wisdom of God.

The Word of God will guide your children wherever they go and in whatever they do.

> Thy word is a lamp unto my feet, and a light unto my path. (Psalm 119:105)

The Word of God will secure your children and deliver them from temptations, bad habits, sin and contemptuous ridicule that is all around them.

> Wherewithal shall a young man cleanse his way? By taking heed thereto according to thy word. (Psalm 119:9)

The Word of God will also guard your children against the dangers and the traps of the last days.

> For men shall be lovers of their own selves, covetous, boasters, proud, blasphemers, disobedient to parents, unthankful, unholy without natural affection, truce breakers, false accusers, incontinent, fierce, despisers of those that are good, traitors, heady, high-minded, lovers of pleasures more than lovers of God. Having a form of godliness, but denying the power thereof: from such turn away. (2 Timothy 3:2–5)
>
> He sent his word and healed them, and delivered them from their destructions. (Psalm 107:20)

Dear parent, the Word of God taught to your children will keep them away from the tendency of joining bad company, getting involved in gangs, or dealing in drugs or any other vice that may derail their glorious destiny.

> He taught me also and said unto me. Let thine heart retain my words: Keep my commandments and live.

> Get wisdom, get understanding: forget it not; neither decline from the words of my mouth.

> Forsake her not and she shall preserve thee: love her, and she shall keep thee. Wisdom is the principal thing; therefore get wisdom: and with all thy getting get understanding.

> Exalt her, and she shall promote thee: She shall bring thee to honour, when thou doest embrace her.

> She shall give to thine head an ornament of grace: a crown of glory shall she deliver to thee.

> Hear, O my son, and receive my sayings, and the years of thy life shall be many. (Proverbs 4:4–10)

When you teach your children the Word of God, you are sowing the seeds of greatness, protection, deliverance, preservation, honour, and above all, the seeds of success and advantage.

2. Your Decision to Be United as a Family

> And Jesus knew their thoughts, and said unto them, every kingdom divided against itself is brought to desolation; and every city or house divided against itself shall not stand. (Matthew 12:25)

> Behold, how good and how pleasant it is for brethren to dwell together in unity . . . for there the Lord commanded the blessing, even life for evermore. (Psalm 133:1–3)

> And the whole earth was of one language and of one speech. And it came to pass, as they journeyed from

east, that they found a plain in the land of Shinar, and they dwelt there. And they said one to another, Go to, let us make brick, and burn them thoroughly. And they had brick for stone, and slime had they for mortar.

And they said, go to, let us build us city and a tower, whose top may reach unto heaven; and let us make us a name, lest we be scattered abroad upon the face of the whole earth. And the LORD came down to see the city and the tower, which the children of men built.

And the LORD said, Behold the people is one, and they have one language; and this they begin to do: and now nothing will be restrained from them, which they have imagined to do. (Genesis 11:1–6)

A strong home or a nation is the one that is united in purpose, vision, and language. Consider nations like the United States of America and the United Kingdom. These nations are powerful and influential on earth not because they are the most populated or naturally endowed nations on the planet Earth but because the families in these nations are united and have a common language. They are democratic and united behind a common vision and values. It is apparent that these nations and the people command blessings. They are progressive and more prosperous in contrast to some of the nations in Africa, where the people speak different languages and are united merely behind ethnic and tribal lines, with each tribe having its own chief or ruler. Even though these nations may adopt democracy as a way of government, often times they struggle to reach a consensus. These nations with so much natural resources and human resources are oftentimes some of the poorest nations on earth.

A close examination of the lives of the people may reveal high levels of suspicion, division, and enmity. Some of the atrocities and genocides committed in the world are apparent in these nations because when there is no vision, the people perish. Some of the social and political challenges facing some nations of the world such as poverty, famine , civil wars, political upheavals, and terrorism, have its root causes in disunity and lack of common vision for the development of the people of the nations. These challenges often are rooted in families and tribes that perpetually sow seeds of divisions and perceive the 'other' as an enemy.

Sadly, these nations become vulnerable and, oftentimes, the theatre where poverty, disease, and corruption thrive to the detriment of its people. The people are hence compelled to seek shelter and asylum in nations where they know there is progress and development.

Recently, we see these phenomena in the news where these people are forced to embark on perilous journeys across the Atlantic Ocean in search of a desired haven.

It is recognised that when there is unity, a tremendous spiritual, mental, and physical energy is unleashed for progressive development and growth. This spiritual energy and capability is a blessing from God that makes possible the aspirations and the visions of the people regardless of the prevailing conditions in the world.

It is vital to emphasise that whatever you intend to build as a family must bring glory to God and must transform the earth and make it a better place for humanity to live and thrive. It must be based on eternal and timeless values of peace, hope, and love.

3. Your Decision to Pray for Your Family Always

> And Aaron shall bear the names of the children of Israel in the breastplate of judgement upon his heart, when he goeth in unto the holy place, for a memorial before the LORD continually. (Exodus 28:29)

> Moreover as for me, God forbid that I should sin against the LORD in ceasing to pray for you: but I will teach you the good and the right way: Only fear the LORD, and serve him in truth with all your heart: for consider how great things he hath done for you. (1 Samuel 12:23–24)

> Evening, and morning, and at noon, will I pray, and cry aloud: and he shall hear my voice. He hath delivered my soul in peace from the battle that was against me: for there were many with me. (Psalm 55:17–18)

Prayer must be based on a loving relationship with our heavenly Father and must be based on the knowledge that Jesus Christ, the only begotten Son of God, has fully paid the price by His vicarious death on the cross at Calvary, and so we are justified by grace to come boldly to His presence in the name of Jesus Christ to petition God to intervene in the lives of our loved ones and family.

The effectual fervent prayer of the righteous man avails much because your prayers unleash ministering angels to carry the Word of God to the circumstances surrounding you and to ensure that the will of God comes to pass in your life and those you pray for.

An example of a biblical character who prayed for his family is the patriarch Abraham.

> And the LORD said, shall I hide from Abraham that thing which I do; Seeing that Abraham shall surely become great and mighty nation, and all the nations of the Earth shall be blessed in him?
>
> For I know him, that he will command his children and his household after him, and they shall keep the way of the LORD, to do justice and judgement, that the LORD may bring upon Abraham that which he hath spoken of him . . . but Abraham stood yet before the LORD and Abraham drew near, and said, Wilt thou also destroy the righteous with the wicked? (Genesis 18:17–23)

In the above scriptural reference, we see the father of faith as a role model of someone who cares enough to draw near to the creator of the universe in prayer of intercession.

God also bears record of him that he will command his children and his household after him, and they shall keep the way of the Lord.

It is urgent that fathers and mothers take time to seek counsel from the word of God and spend time in prayer for their family.

Let us further be encouraged by the following scripture on prayer to facilitate and pray constantly for each member of our families.

> Therefore, make it your habit to confess your sins to one another and to pray for one another, so that you may be healed. The prayer of a righteous person is powerful and effective. (James 5:16)

> Praying always with all prayer and supplication in the Spirit, and watching thereunto with all perseverance and supplication for all saints. (Ephesians 6:18)

> Then Abraham prayed to God, and God healed Abimelek, his wife and his female slaves so they could have children again. (Genesis 20:17)

> Again I say to you, that if two of you agree on Earth about anything that they may ask, it shall be done for them by my Father who is in heaven. For where two or three have gathered together in my name, I am there in their midst. (Matthew 18:19–20)

4. Your Decision to Have a Vision for Your Family

> Where there is no vision the people perish: but he that kept the law, is happy. (Proverbs 29:18)

> I will stand upon my watch, and set me upon the tower, and will watch to see what he will say unto me, and what I shall answer when I am reproved. And the Lord answer me and said; write the vision and make it plain upon tables, that he may run that readeth it. For the vision is yet for an appointed time, but at the end it shall speak, and not lie: though it tarry, wait for it because it will surely come, it will not tarry. (Habakkuk 2:1–3)

After these things the word of the word of the Lord came unto Abram in a vision saying, fear not, Abram: I am thy shield and thy exceeding great reward. And Abram said, Lord God, what wilt thou give me, seeing I go childless . . . but he that shall come forth out of thine own bowels shall be thine heir. And He brought him forth abroad, and said, look now toward heaven and tell the stars, if thou be able to number them: and he said unto him, so shall thy seed be and he believed in the Lord; and He counted it to him for righteousness. (Genesis 15:1–6)

And God spake unto Israel in the visions of the night and said, Jacob, Jacob and he said here am I. And He said I am God, the God of thy father: fear not to go down into Egypt, for I will there make of thee a great nation: I will go down with thee into Egypt and I will also surely bring thee up again: And Joseph shall put his hand upon thine eyes. And Jacob rose up from Beersheba: and the sons of Israel carried Jacob their father and their little ones, and their wives, in the wagons which Pharaoh had sent to carry him. (Genesis 46:2–5)

And thine house and thy kingdom shall be established forever before thee: thy throne shall be established forever. according to all these words, and according to all this vision, so did Nathan speak unto David. (2 Samuel 7:16–17)

According to the custom of the priest's office, his lot was to burn incense when he went into the temple of the Lord. And the multitude of the people were praying without at the time of incense. And there appeared unto him an angel of the Lord standing on the right side of the altar of incense.

And when Zacharias saw him, he was troubled, and fear fell upon him. But the angel said unto him, 'Fear not, Zacharias: for thy prayer is heard and thy wife Elizabeth shall bear thee a son, and thou shall call him name John.

> And thou shalt have joy and gladness; and many shall rejoice at his birth. For he shall be great in the sight of the Lord and shall drink neither wine nor strong drink; and he shall be filled with the Holy Ghost, even from his mother's womb. And he shall go before him in the spirit and power of Elias, to turn the hearts of fathers to the children, and the disobedient to the wisdom of the just; to make ready a people prepared for the Lord'. (Luke 1:9–17)

If your family will experience uncommon success in any chosen area or sphere, then it is vital that there is clear revelation or vision regarding that particular area or vocation. There is the need to pursue the knowledge and insights through diligence and deliberate practice.

When you have a vision concerning your future, then there is a reason for living. Vision which is documented and displayed will help you to devise strategic plans towards its fulfilment. Then work on your plans and remain focused till you achieve your goals and then keep doing this till your vision become a reality.

When the vision is clear, then it will generate within you the necessary passion and motivation to move from little to maximum and from nowhere to somewhere to see the fulfilment of that vision. When your vision becomes an obsession, then nothing is capable of stopping you or your household. The rest is a matter of time.

Anytime I read about uncommon achievements and/or people that the media refer to as 'stars', I see an individual or a family with a clear vision of where they are going and what they want to achieve. They are committed to excellence at whatever cost. No wonder they shine in their chosen areas.

The Bible is full of visionaries whose ordinary lives became extraordinary and exemplary as a result of vision. As a result, we are encouraged to have a vision and write the vision down. When a vision is written down and pursued, then the vision now begins to speak and draw all the necessary resources towards its fulfilment.

The establishment of any house and destiny depends on how clear the vision for the house or destiny is and how the vision speaks.

When there is no vision, the people perish. The people are going nowhere. They are static. I pray for you today that you will have a vision for your life and your family—a vision that will fulfil the original purpose of God for your life and your family and nation in Jesus' name.

When there is no vision, life has no meaning. Frustration, tiredness, boredom, and stress set in. Sometimes you are prone to all negative emotions and tendencies because there is no vision. There is chaos, waste, and a persistent sense of hopelessness and despair. When there is vision, there will be provisions. What you see is what you get.

Where are you now? What do you have now? Who have you become? Whatever your answers are, they can all be traced to the visions you had in the past. Now you can go higher and do greater things if you have the courage and the tenacity to receive the vision of God for your life and family.

Ask the Lord in prayer to reveal to you what He would have you do for the rest of your life. Ask God to give you a vision for your family. God is the giver of every good and perfect gift, and when God wants to bless you above all that you can think or imagine, God will give you a vision or a dream that is bigger than your present experience. God did it for Abraham, Jacob, and Daniel. God did it for Paul and Joseph. God will do it for you too.

5. Your Decision to Pursue Knowledge

> My people are destroyed for lack of knowledge: because thou has rejected knowledge. I will also reject thee, that thou shalt be no priest to me: seeing thou has forgotten the law of thy God, I will also forget thy children. (Hosea 4:6)

> Wise men layup knowledge: but the mouth of the foolish is near destruction. (Proverbs 10:14)

> The fear of the Lord is the beginning of wisdom: and the knowledge of the holy is understanding.
>
> For by me thy days shall be multiplied and the years of thy life shall be increased. (Proverbs 9:11)
>
> The lips of the wise disperse knowledge: but the heart of the foolish does not so. (Proverbs 15:7)
>
> Then shall they call upon me but I will not answer; they shall seek me early, but they shall not find me:
>
> For that they hated knowledge, and did not choose the fear of the Lord. (Proverbs 1:28–29)
>
> In the first year of his reign, I Daniel understood by books the number of years, whereof the word of the Lord came to Jeremiah the prophet, that he would accomplish seventy years in the destructions of Jerusalem.
>
> And I set my face unto the Lord God, to seek by prayer and supplications, with fasting and sackcloth and ashes (Daniel 9:2–3)
>
> Till I come, give attendance to the reading, to exhortation, to doctrine. (1 Timothy 4:13)
>
> Study to show thyself approved unto God, a workman that needeth not to be ashamed, rightly dividing the word of truth. (1 Timothy 2:15)

Knowledge is capable of transforming your current circumstance. Knowledge which is acted upon can make available a tremendous power capable of changing for the better the prevailing situation.

> But the people that do know their God shall be strong and do exploits. (Daniel 11:32b)

GILBERT GBEDAWO

Just look at Adam and Eve in the Garden of Eden before Eve was deceived by the old serpent—the Devil. Adam single-handedly named all the animals. He was a genius and did some scientific and mind-boggling exploits. He was strong and in charge of a vast real estate. He knew the voice of God and communicated with the Creator till he was deceived and lost fellowship with the Creator.

However, when they ignored the laws of God and disobeyed His instructions, they became weak, fearful, and disempowered. The devil became their master and the god of the world. They were evicted from the garden and they lost their true identity.

Therefore, when you make up your mind to pursue God, know Him intimately, and follow his ways of doing things through the study of His Word (the Bible), you become a candidate to receive strength and do exploits—great works. Jesus put it this way:

> Very truly I tell you, whoever believes in me will do the works I have been doing, and they will do even greater works than these, because I am going to the Father. (John 14:12)

> But thou, O Daniel, shut up the words, and seal the book, even to the time of the end: many shall run to and fro, and knowledge shall be increased. (Daniel 12:4)

> And this entire vision has become for you like the words of a sealed book. When people give it to someone who can read and say, 'Read this please,' he answers, 'I cannot, because it is sealed.' (Isaiah 29:11)

> He replied, 'Because the knowledge of the secrets of the kingdom of Heaven has been given to you, but not to them.' (Matthew 13:11)

Our libraries, schools, national archives, universities, and research institutions are full of books. Every year, new books are published. Every month, there are new research findings that are published in journals. Every week, there are thousands of expositions and

STEPS TOWARDS EDUCATIONAL EXCELLENCE

sermons being preached in various churches. It is vital that we apply the truths in the Word of God, coupled with the latest discoveries in the field of our expertise, to do greater works and to ensure that we spread the goodness of God to every person on earth. We push back darkness in its various forms—disease, sin, oppression, exploitation, poverty, social and economic dislocation, and spiritual famine—that have engulfed the world.

We must do everything to ensure that the kingdoms of this world become the kingdom of our heavenly Father and Christ Jesus through the knowledge of God, and we must take hold on the assignment of God to occupy till He comes. It is time to work while it is day, for when night comes, no man can work.

We must always invest in our personal library and the library of our children. We must identify and purchase the right books that will enhance our knowledge and help us to do excellent work in every facet of our lives. We must always be informed and keep up with the relevant information that will empower us to reach new and greater heights.

Our children must see us reading, and we must encourage and promote the culture of reading at home. We must ensure that they understand what they read through writing book reviews and discussions at home.

We must start with the Bible and continue with their schoolbooks and other books of interest to them. They must read the newspaper as well to know current affairs and possibly discuss how they would tackle some of the issues raised in these newspapers if they are in position to do so. In conclusion, let us be reminded by the words in the following scripture:

> Buy the truth and sell it not; also wisdom and instruction and understanding. (Proverbs 23:23)

> And further, by these my son be admonished of making many books there is no end; and much study is a weariness of the flesh.

Let us hear the conclusion of the whole matter: Fear God, keep his commandments: for this is the whole duty of man.

For God shall bring every work into judgement, with every secret thing whether it be good or whether it be evil. (Ecclesiastes 12:12-14)

Study to show thyself approved unto God, a workman that needed not to be ashamed, rightly dividing the word of truth. (2 Timothy 2:15)

6. Your Decision to Honour Your Parents and All Men

Honour thy father and thy mother that thy days may be long upon the land which the Lord thy God giveth thee. (Exodus 20:12)

Children, obey your parents in the Lord: for this is right. Honour thy father and mother; (which is the first commandment with a promise) that it may be well with thee, and thou mayest live long on the earth.

And ye fathers provoke not your children to wrath: but bring them up in the nurture and admonition of the Lord.

Servants, be obedient to them that are your masters according to the flesh with fear and trembling in singleness of your heart as unto Christ.

Not with eye service as men pleasers, but as the servants of Christ doing the will of God from the heart;

With good will doing service, as to the Lord and not to men:

Knowing that whatsoever good thing any man doeth the same shall he receive of the Lord, whether he be bond or free.

> And ye masters do the same things unto the, forbearing threatening: knowing that your Master also is in heaven neither is there respect of persons with Him. (Ephesians 6:2–9)
>
> Honour thy father and thy mother: and thou shalt love thy neighbour as thyself. (Matthew 19:19)

Honour is a major currency that guarantees longevity, favour, protection, and well-being.

The Bible is full of men and women who have chosen the path of honour. These men and women receive in return the ability to live long, productive, fulfilled, blessed, and inspiring lives. There are those who sow the seeds of dishonour and equally reap the consequences of their actions. Their actions can also affect future generations as the sins of the forefathers are passed down to the fourth generation.

Indeed, honour must first become a seed before it can ever become a harvest in your life. The scripture confirms or declares this in Genesis 8:22:

> While the earth remaineth, seed time and harvest . . . shall not cease.

Precious reader, you can choose how long you will live on earth and the blessings you will receive by paying a close attention to Exodus 20:12

Honour thy father and thy mother: that thy days may be long upon the land which the LORD thy God giveth thee.

Honour thy father and mother, (which is the first commandment with promise) that it may be well with thee, and thou mayest live long on the earth. And ye fathers, provoke not your children to wrath: but bring them up in the nurture and admonition of the Lord. (Ephesians 6:2–4)

Honouring your parents, teachers, and indeed all men will unleash a tirade of favour and grace as you have never experienced before.

Get ready to experience promotion and elevation in your family and community. Get ready to move into greater joy and destiny because you have decided to sow the seeds of honour.

Think about the biblical character called Joseph. Joseph honoured his parents, brothers, Portiphar, the butler, the baker, and also the pharaoh. Initially, it appeared as though he was going down, but remember, a seed must first go down into the soil and die to itself before bringing forth a new plant. Joseph experienced opposition and betrayal even from those he honoured, but at the fullness of time, the appointed time, he was remembered by God and lifted to the place of honour as the prime minister of Egypt, the superpower of those days.

Another great example is Jesus. As a child growing up, He knew who He was: God's only begotten Son. Yet He also sowed seeds of honour. Initially, it appeared that the only reward of honouring people was death, but guess what? God raised Him up from the grave and has given Him a name that is far greater and better than any other name: Jesus Christ.

When you choose to honour people, sometimes it may appear as if you were losing. But wait, a glorious change is coming your way, and in the fullness of time, you will receive more than you have given.

Do not give up! Do not give in! A change of season is coming, and a harvest of honour is coming your way.

7. Your Decision to Have the Right Attitude

I have heard it said that your attitude determines your altitude. In other words, your attitude towards life and people will ultimately position you for failure or success. It will determine the degree of success, especially in your job, business, and home.

Many people live life comparing themselves to others and measuring themselves by the standards others have set in their network or sphere of influence or society. These attitudes determine how far these people may go. The grass always looks greener elsewhere, but take a minute to consider the words of David in Psalm 23.

> The Lord is my shepherd (to feed, guide, and shield me), I shall not lack. He makes me lie down in green (fresh, tender) pastures; He leads me beside the still and restful waters. He refreshes and restores my life (myself); He leads me in the paths of righteousness (uprightness and right standing with Him—not for my earning it, but) for his name's sake.
>
> You prepare a table before me in the presence of my enemies. You anoint my head with oil; my (brimming) cup runs over. Surely (or only) goodness, mercy and unfailing love shall follow me all the days of my life, and through the length of my days, the house of the Lord and his presence shall be my dwelling place.

In Psalm 23, David encourages us to know the Lord as our shepherd who provides, feeds, guides, and shields us from the dangers and uncertainties of the prevailing social and economic climate.

We must look beyond the circumstances and the dark clouds that from time to time try to block the beautiful beam of light that illuminates our days.

At one point or another, every family will face a scenario which may threaten their joy and peace. For some families, it may be a health issue (a sickness or disease) that attacks a member of the family. For others, it may be a sudden loss of a loved one. And for others, it may be a sudden termination of employment or contract or a financial crisis. But dear reader, whatever forms the storms of life may take, know that the Lord is your shepherd, and therefore, you will not lack any good thing.

GILBERT GBEDAWO

The storm will pass away, and you will still be here because you are not alone. After every devastation caused by the storm, your soul and mind will be restored and renewed, and you will testify to the goodness of the Lord because He promised never to leave you nor forsake you regardless of the situation as long as you believe Him.

In spite of what you have gone through in the past, you are still here, and despite what life may throw at you, I know and believe that you and your household will come out stronger and better. It is therefore imperative that we keep the right attitude when we are confronted with trials and the testing of our faith. Our anchor must hold in the storms of life.

Look at Psalm 34:19:

> The righteous person faces many troubles, but the Lord comes to the rescue each time.

> Many are the afflictions of the righteous but the Lord delivers him out of them all.

> What do you imagine against the Lord, he will make and utter end: affliction shall not rise up the second time. (Nahum 1:9)

CHAPTER 10

Getting to Know Your Child

For unto us a child is born, unto us a son is given, and the government shall be upon His shoulder: and His name shall be called Wonderful, Counselor, Mighty God, Everlasting Father, Prince of Peace.

> Of the increase of his government and peace, there shall be no end, upon the throne of David, and upon his kingdom, to order it, and to establish it with judgement and with justice from henceforth even forever. The zeal of the Lord of hosts will perform this. (Isaiah 9:6–7)

> And there went a man of the house of Levi, and took to wife a daughter of Levi. And the woman conceived and bare a son: and when she saw him that he was a goodly child, she hid him three months.

> And when she could no longer hide him, she took for him an ark of bulrushes, and doubled it with slime and with pitch and put the child therein and she laid it in the flags by the rivers brink. And his sister stood afar off, to wit what would be done to him. (Exodus 2:1–4)

> And a little child shall lead them. (Isaiah 11:6b)

Now Israel loved Joseph more than all his children, because he was the son of his old age: and he made him a coat of many colours. (Isaiah 37:3)

Lo, children are an heritage of the Lord; and the fruit of the womb is his reward.

As arrows are in the hand of a mighty man; so are children of the youth.

Happy is the man that hath his quiver full of them: they shall not be ashamed but they shall speak with the enemies in the gate. (Psalm 127:3–5)

Thy wife shall be as a fruitful vine by the sides of thine house: thy children like olive plants round about thy table. Behold that thus shall the man be blessed that feareth the Lord. (Psalm 128:3–4)

Even a child is known by his doings, whether his work be pure, and whether it be right. (Proverbs 20:11)

The rod and reproof give wisdom: but a child left to himself bringeth his mother to shame. (Proverbs 29:15)

Correct thy son, and he shall give thee rest; yea he shall give delight into thy soul. (Proverbs 29:17)

Take heed that ye despite not one of these little ones (children); for I say unto you, that in heaven their angels do always behold the face of my Father which is in heaven. (Matthew 18:10)

Let no man despise thy youth; but be thou an example of the believers, in word, in conversation, in charity, in spirit, in faith, in purity. (1 Timothy 4:12)

The powerful truth about every child is that every child is unique. A child may resemble and take on some physical traits of siblings, but in terms of skills, talents, dispositions, endowments, and gifting, each child is unique and special.

It is vital for parents and caregivers to celebrate the uniqueness of every child and to plan for the development and training of the child so that each child can flourish and reach his or her full potential in life.

Some children from an early age demonstrate certain capabilities that may serve as indicators of their unique pathway to stardom, career, and calling.

Through critical observation and interaction with children, parents can identify the interests, aspirations, hopes, and dreams of their children.

Sometimes external agencies, such as educational institutions or churches and/or faith groups, may spot some of these unique abilities. Other times, a sports club or an independent observer may discover the potential of a child.

Whatever form this may take, parents must be aware of how unique and special a child is and make the necessary investment of time and finances to help develop and train the child in question.

It is paramount as parents and guardians to observe our children's interests and hobbies as therein might lie their purpose in life. Once this observation has been made, deliberate steps can be taken to nurture and further develop these hobbies and interests into a plausible career path for the child, should they excel in it.

Then the Word of the Lord came unto me, saying:

> Before I formed thee in the belly, I knew thee, and before thou camest forth out of the womb I sanctified thee, and ordained thee a prophet unto the nations. Then said I, Ah, Lord God! Behold I cannot speak: for I am a child. (Jeremiah 1:4–6)

The above scripture denotes that before a child is born, God already has a plan and a purpose.

Sometimes, children are born out of wedlock or without any major plan, but in spite of the circumstances that may surround the birth, it is worth remembering that there is a higher and divine agenda for every child that makes it through to this beautiful earth.

This is what the Lord, the Holy One of Israel, and your creator says: 'Do you question what I do for my children? Do you give me orders about the work of my hands?' (Isaiah 45:11).

Sometimes there appears to be a conflict between what children want to do and what parents want to have them do. It is necessary to pray and ask for counsel and advice in such times so that the original purpose of God for the children is not derailed or jeopardised due to the wishes and aspirations of the parents. However, it is crucial to ensure that parental input and responsibility are not subjugated.

Parents should support, advise, and guide their children in both minor and major decisions, bearing in mind that

> many are the plans in a man's heart but it is the counsel of God that would stand.

> You can make many plans but the Lord's purpose will prevail. (Proverbs 19:21)

> There are many devices in a man's heart nevertheless the counsel of the Lord that shall stand. (Proverbs 19:21, KJV)

Sometimes children are coerced to choose a particular programme of study. For example, parents want the child to choose a science programme with the intention that the child will eventually pursue medical science and graduate as a medical doctor, whereas that child was gifted to be a social worker or a human rights activist or a pianist or an entrepreneur or an actor or a musician or a politician or a business executive, to mention but a few.

I pray for you that the wisdom and counsel of God will come upon you as you help your child make the decisions of what subjects to study and career path to choose.

I also pray that the original counsel of God for your child will stand in the precious name of Jesus Christ.

> A man's gift maketh room for him, and bringeth him before great men. (Proverbs 18:16)

God has placed gifts in your child that have the potential to make them great.

It is essential that you do not neglect or despise that gift but begin to protect, develop, and allow your child to use his/her gift to bless others.

The world is about to pay for the expression of the gift within you. The world is waiting to celebrate the gift that your child is developing and working on.

Something great and beautiful is about to happen in the life of your children as you encourage and celebrate the unique gift they exhibit.

The Seven Things Every Parent Should Know about Their Children

Knowledge is fundamental for transformation, growth, and progress. It is believed that we are now in a knowledge economy, and every day, new frontiers of knowledge are being discovered. It is popularly claimed that knowledge is power, but I differ a bit on this saying. I always believe that knowledge which is applied and aimed at a problem with the view of providing solution is powerful as power is the rate at which work is done.

There is no use just accumulating information or knowledge if it will not be applied to advance our families and make the society a better place for children to flourish. In this section, let us consider seven things every parent should know about their children.

GILBERT GBEDAWO

1. **Your Children Are a Reward from God, and They Matter to Him**

> Lo, children are a heritage of the LORD: and the fruit of the womb is his reward. (Psalm 127:3)

> Before I formed thee in the belly I knew thee: and before thou camest forth out of the womb I sanctified thee, and I ordained thee a prophet unto the nations. (Jeremiah 1:5)

> And the LORD said unto her, two nations are in thy womb, and two manner of people shall be separated from thy bowels; and the one people shall be stronger than the other people; and the elder shall serve the younger, and when her days to be delivered were fulfilled, behold, there were twins in her womb. (Genesis 25:23–24)

> Behold, I and the children whom the LORD hath given me are for signs and for wonders in Israel from the LORD of hosts, which dwelled in mount Zion. And when they shall say unto you, Seek unto them that have familiar spirits, and unto wizards that peep, and that mutter: should not a people seek unto their God for the living to the dead? (Isaiah 8:18)

> And the sucking child shall play on the hole of the asp, and the weaned child shall put his hand on the cockatrice's den.

> They shall not hurt nor destroy in all my holy mountain: for the earth shall be full of the knowledge of the LORD, as the waters cover the sea.

> And in that day there shall be a root of Jesse, which shall stand for an ensign of the people; to it shall the Gentiles seek: and his rest shall be glorious. (Isaiah 11:8–10)

> Didn't the LORD make you one with your wife? In body and spirit you are his. And what does he want? Godly

children from your union. So guard your heart; remain loyal to the wife of your youth. (Malachi 2:15, NLT)

Through the offspring the LORD gives you by this young woman, may your family be like that of Perez, whom Tamar bore to Judah. (Ruth 4:12)

Eli would bless Elkanah and his wife, saying, 'May the LORD give you children by this woman to take the place of the one she prayed for and gave to the LORD.' Then they would go home. (1 Samuel 2:20)

When you are rewarded with children, it is required and expected that you cherish, protect and value the children you are blessed with. These children are special and unique. They are packaged for success and greatness. It is my hope that you cherish them and nurture them to achieve their full potential.

2. You Must Discover the Gifts, Talents, Passions, Dreams, and Aspirations of Your Children and Invest in Them

Every good and perfect gift is from above, coming down from the Father of the heavenly lights, who does not change like shifting shadows. (James 1:17)

To this John replied, 'A person can receive only what is given them from heaven.' (John 3:27)

And unto one he gave five talents, to another two, and to another one; to every man according to his several ability; and straightway took his journey. (Matthew 25:15)

And I have filled him with the Spirit of God, with wisdom, with understanding, with knowledge and with all kinds of skills. (Exodus 31:3)

We have different gifts, according to the grace given to each of us. If your gift is prophesying, then prophesy in accordance with your faith. (Romans 12:6)

GILBERT GBEDAWO

> I wish that all of you were as I am. But each of you has your own gift from God; one has this gift, another has that. (1 Corinthians 7:7)

> Wherefore he saith, when he ascended up on high, he led captivity captive, and gave gifts unto men. (Ephesians 4:8)

> And when his parents saw him, they were astonished. And his mother said to him, 'Son, why have you treated us so? Behold, your father and I have been searching for you in great distress.

> And he said to them, 'Why were you looking for me? Did you not know that I must be in my Father's house?' (Luke 2:48–49)

> I must do the work of the one who sent me while it is day. Night is approaching, when no one can work. (John 9:4)

> For this reason I remind you to fan into flame the gift of God, which is in you through the laying on of my hands. (2 Timothy 1:6)

The truth I want to emphasise here is that every child is different in terms of their abilities, gifts, callings, passions, dispositions, talents, and drives. It is the duty of parents to know the unique ability sets that make one child different from the other and to develop an action plan to help nurture the dreams and aspirations of each child so that, as individuals in a family, each of your children can thrive and flourish and be themselves. Parents must avoid the temptation of comparing one child with the other or preferring one child above the other.

This breeds sibling rivalry, where children are all the time competing with one another in a vain attempt to please their parents. Children must be valued and made to understand that they are unique and special. Parents should always endeavor to create an atmosphere of love and respect for every member of the family unit. Training in the wisdom of God is essential to promote family cohesion and unity.

After you have discovered the unique abilities of your children, every effort should be made to go the extra mile, and invest your time and financial resources to nurture and develop the talents they possess. When we see children who have become successful, it is apparent that a parent, a close relative, or a mentor took time to train the child.

3. Every Parent Should Know the Close Friends of Their Children

> A man of many companions may come to ruin, but there is a friend who sticks closer than a brother. (Proverbs 18:24)

> Do not make friends with a hot-tempered man, do not associate with one easily angered, or you may learn his ways and get yourself ensnared. (Proverbs 22:24–25)

> He who walks with the wise grows wise, but a companion of fools suffers harm. (Proverbs 13:20)

> Two are better than one, because they have a good return for their work: If one falls down, his friend can help him up. But pity the man who falls and has no one to help him up! (Ecclesiastes 4:9–10)

> A friend loves at all times, and a brother is born for adversity. (Proverbs 17:17)

> As iron sharpens iron, so one man sharpens another. (Proverbs 27:17)

> Oh, for the days when I was in my prime, when God's intimate friendship blessed my house, when the Almighty was still with me and my children were around me, when my path was drenched with cream and the rock poured out for me streams of olive oil. (Job 29:4–6)

My intercessor is my friend as my eyes pour out tears to God; on behalf of a man he pleads with God as a man pleads for his friend. (Job 16:20–21)

> You adulterous people, don't you know that friendship with the world is hatred toward God? Anyone who chooses to be a friend of the world becomes an enemy of God. (James 4:4)

It is vital for parents to know and be thoroughly satisfied with the close friends of their children. The reason is that friends are capable of motivating one another towards excellent ideals and good works or otherwise. Some friendships can promote the well-being of those involved and result in academic excellence, while others can ruin the lives of the people involved.

During my secondary education days, in a boarding school, I saw the effects of bad friendships and the devastating consequences on the educational outcome of those involved. Likewise, I have been privileged to learn from some very good friendships which serve as a motivation to study hard and make progress. When parents provide guidance and keep watch on the type of friends their children get involved with, I think it will positively affect the outcomes of their learning and growth.

4. Every Parent Must Know What Their Children Are Learning at School

> Be diligent to know the state of your flocks, and look well to your herds. (Proverbs 27:23)
>
> Learn to do well; seek judgment, relieve the oppressed, judge the fatherless, plead for the widow. (Isaiah 1:17)
>
> Put your outdoor work in order and get your fields ready; after that, build your house. (Proverbs 24:27)
>
> Son of man, prophesy against the shepherds of Israel; prophesy and say to them: 'This is what the Sovereign LORD says: Woe to you shepherds of Israel who only take

> care of yourselves! Should not shepherds take care of the flock?' (Ezekiel 34:2)
>
> I will place over them one shepherd, my servant David, and he will tend them; he will tend them and be their shepherd. (Ezekiel 34:23)
>
> He has showed you, O man, what is good; and what does the LORD require of you, but to do justly, and to love mercy, and to walk humbly with your God? (Micah 6:8)
>
> Train up a child in the way he should go: and when he is old, he will not depart from it. (Proverbs 22:6)

Parents must find out daily what their children are learning at school as soon as they have the opportunity. It will give you an idea about the hours they spend in school and whether they are well utilised. Ask your child questions regarding the various subjects they are learning. Ask them to describe the lesson and how it was delivered. Ask them whether they understood the lesson or not. Find out how they contributed to the learning. Ask about their classwork and notebooks. Find out if they have homework, and check to see if it is well done before it is presented.

Find out what they will be learning the next day and week. Monitor the progress continuously. Find out from the school teacher what you can do as a parent to support your children's learning at home. Enquire about the textbooks and recommended reading list for your child.

Invest in your children's extra learning or tutoring. It will be best to have a conversation with your child to determine the areas he or she is struggling to cope with at school and put in the necessary remedies. Do not wait till your child is preparing to sit an exam. Find out early. Develop a timetable for your child, and hold him or her accountable for it.

Create a quiet learning zone at home for studies, and be interested in what they are learning. If you do not have the time to do this, invest in a tutor to take care of this and report regularly to you.

It has been shown time and again that when parents get involved with the school that their children attend, the children do well in school and go on to better schools and excel in education and later in life.

It is imperative that parents get to know exactly what their children are learning at school by cooperating with the teachers at school. Build a positive relationship with the school so that your child can be supported and encouraged to reach his or her full potential because your child matters. One of the ways to do this is by attending parents' evenings to discuss the progress of your child and by attending other meetings targeted at parents. Also, volunteer your time when needed by the school. Whatever you do, get a grip on your child's learning because successful parents do.

Parents should also create reward systems at home to encourage hard work at school. The children must be aware of how they will be rewarded at home when they excel in school and in studies. This will reinforce and boost their morale. I would like each parent to think and discuss with their children what these rewards should be. The children should know and enjoy the rewards of excellence and diligence, and in this way, they will be motivated to become active independent learners.

5. Every Parent Should Know and Deal with the Fears, Concerns and Personal Struggles of their Children Through Engagement and Dialogue

> Fear thou not; for I am with thee: be not dismayed; for I am thy God: I will strengthen thee; yea, I will help thee; yea, I will uphold thee with the right hand of my righteousness. (Isaiah 41:10)

> Be careful for nothing; but in everything by prayer and supplication with thanksgiving let your requests be made known unto God. (Philippians 4:6–7)

What time I am afraid, I will trust in thee. (Psalm 56:3)

For God hath not given us the spirit of fear; but of power, and of love, and of a sound mind. (2 Timothy 1:7)

Therefore I say unto you, Take no thought for your life, what ye shall eat, or what ye shall drink; nor yet for your body, what ye shall put on. Is not the life more than meat, and the body than raiment? (Matthew 6:25–34)

Be strong and of a good courage, fear not, nor be afraid of them: for the LORD thy God, he [it is] that doth go with thee; he will not fail thee, nor forsake thee. (Deuteronomy 31:6)

I sought the LORD, and he heard me, and delivered me from all my fears. (Psalm 34:4)

Humble yourselves therefore under the mighty hand of God, that he may exalt you in due time. (1 Peter 5:6–7)

Casting all your care upon him; for he careth for you. (1 Peter 5:7)

There is no fear in love; but perfect love casteth out fear: because fear hath torment. He that feareth is not made perfect in love. (1 John 4:18)

Have not I commanded thee? Be strong and of a good courage; be not afraid, neither be thou dismayed: for the LORD thy God [is] with thee whithersoever thou goest. (Joshua 1:9)

Say to them [that are] of a fearful heart, Be strong, fear not: behold, your God will come [with] vengeance, [even] God [with] a recompense; he will come and save you. (Isaiah 35:4)

GILBERT GBEDAWO

> Peace I leave with you, my peace I give unto you: not as the world giveth, give I unto you. Let not your heart be troubled, neither let it be afraid. (John 14:27)

> Heaviness in the heart of man maketh it stoop: but a good word maketh it glad. (Proverbs 12:25)

> Yea, though I walk through the valley of the shadow of death, I will fear no evil: for thou [art] with me; thy rod and thy staff they comfort me. (Psalm 23:4)

> Take therefore no thought for the morrow: for the morrow shall take thought for the things of itself. Sufficient unto the day [is] the evil thereof. (Matthew 6:34)

> The LORD [is] my light and my salvation; whom shall I fear? the LORD [is] the strength of my life; of whom shall I be afraid? (Psalm 27:1)

When children grow and engage with the outside world in their schools, communities, and sometimes in the nations they live in, they may witness or be exposed to certain behaviours, attitudes, or situations that may make them anxious or fearful. In moments like this, parents should reassure and encourage their children. Children must be made to understand that parental love is unconditional and will always be there to guide and steer them in life.

When children feel vulnerable out there in the society, they must come home, knowing there is a supportive parent who cares for their well-being and will protect them from any form of harm.

If there is an internal or domestic problem that threatens the peace and the well-being of the child, then the recommendation here is to seek help and support by reaching out to social workers and the structures put in place by the government and the society to support children and families faced with child abuse or neglect.

Penny Tassoni et al. (2007) noted that 'it is a sad fact that some children and young people are badly let down or ill-treated by the adults around them. The statistics for abuse make for difficult reading and the consequences of abuse for many children and young people last a lifetime.'

There is no need to suffer in silence and pretend things will turn out right. Reach out and remove anything and everything that is a source of concern to the well-being of your children and your family.

When children feel safe and secure at home and in school, it has a positive effect on learning, and they exhibit good behaviours and build positive relationships.

Parents and, indeed, all teachers must work collaboratively to identify any early signs of neglect and abuse, whether it is emotional abuse, physical abuse, or sexual abuse.

Penny Tassoni et al. (2007: 123) noted the consequences of abuse when they wrote, 'One of the main effects of being abused is emotional damage—children and young people can develop a low sense of self-esteem. They may feel that they are neither valued nor important or even deserving to be valued.'

The long-term possible effects of child abuse noted by Penny Tassoni et al. include but not limited to the following:

- difficulties in forming strong and trusting relationships
- prostitution
- homelessness
- crime
- difficulties in later parenting
- mental health problems
- low achievement in school
- drug and alcohol addictions
- unemployment.

It is crucial that parents and, indeed, all adults working with children and young people take practical steps to combat the menace of child neglect and abuse so that we can have a better society where every child truly matters.

6. Every Parent Should Know about the Educational System and How It Works

> Through wisdom is a house built; and by understanding it is established. (Proverbs 24:3)

> The heart of the discerning acquires knowledge; the ears of the wise seek it out. (Proverbs 18:15)

> The Spirit of the LORD will rest on him, the Spirit of wisdom and of understanding, the Spirit of counsel and of power, the Spirit of knowledge and of the fear of the LORD. (Isaiah 11:2)

> And wisdom and knowledge shall be the stability of thy times, and strength of salvation: the fear of the LORD is his treasure. (Isaiah 33:6)

> Every wise woman buildeth her house: but the foolish plucketh it down with her hands. (Proverbs 14:1)

> Wisdom hath built her house, she hath hewn out her seven pillars. (Proverbs 9:1)

> By the grace God has given me, I laid a foundation as a wise builder, and someone else is building on it. But each one should build with care. (1 Corinthians 3:10)

> And it came to pass, when Solomon had finished the building of the house of the LORD, and the king's house, and all Solomon's desire which he was pleased to do. (1 Kings 9:1)

> It took Solomon thirteen years, however, to complete the construction of his palace. (1 Kings 7:1)

Every parent, especially parents of migrants, should make all efforts to understand the educational system and how it operates so that they can be in a better position to support their children throughout schooling.

My personal experience of dealing with parents who were not originally born in the United Kingdom shows that a lot need to be done in this regard.

Areas of concern include the various key stages, programmes of study, examination types and boards, attainment levels, predicted grades, subjects being learned at school, and the grading system and level descriptors.

Applied knowledge is powerful and key for transformation. Therefore, parents should be familiar with the department for education website (https://www.gov.uk/government/organisations/department-for-education), where they can get the relevant information on the educational system and the current developments regarding education.

Knowing the structure of the educational system and the programme of study will help parents plan adequately for the various stages of the educational development of their children. It will help them to put the right interventions in place to enable each child to reach his or her full potential in school.

I suggest that parents familiarise themselves with the website, www.synergyeducate.com, to learn more and to get further advice on how to support and make the necessary interventions to support the learning of their children.

7. Every Parent Should Know the Key Legislation regarding Their Children

> Where there is no vision, the people perish: but he that keepeth the law, happy is he. (Proverbs 29:18)

> My people are destroyed for lack of knowledge: because thou hast rejected knowledge, I will also reject thee, that thou shalt be no priest to me: seeing thou hast forgotten the law of thy God, I will also forget thy children. (Hosea 4:6)

Foreigners sap his strength, but he does not realize it. His hair is sprinkled with gray, but he does not notice. (Hosea 7:9)

Ephraim is like a dove, easily deceived and senseless— now calling to Egypt, now turning to Assyria. (Hosea 7:11)

Furthermore, it isn't good to be ignorant, and whoever rushes into things misses the mark. (Proverbs 19:2)

And these things will they do unto you, because they have not known the Father, nor me. (John 16:3)

This book of the law shall not depart out of thy mouth; but thou shalt meditate therein day and night, that thou mayest observe to do according to all that is written therein: for then thou shalt make thy way prosperous, and then thou shalt have good success. (Joshua 1:8)

The mouth of the righteous speaketh wisdom, and his tongue talketh of judgment. (Psalm 37:30)

With my lips I recount all the laws that come from your mouth. (Psalm 119:13)

My mouth speaks what is true, for my lips detest wickedness. (Proverbs 8:7)

The mouth of the righteous is a fountain of life, but the mouth of the wicked conceals violence. (Proverbs 10:11)

Wisdom is found on the lips of the discerning, but a rod is for the back of one who has no sense. (Proverbs 10:13)

Penny Tassoni et al. (2007) noted that 'all children have the right to be in a safe and welcoming environment. In the UK there are many pieces of legislation that protect children and their families.' This right is embedded in the notion that 'every child is special and should be given opportunities to fulfil his or her potential'.

Tassoni et al. went further to outline the two significant pieces of legislation that protect children and their families:

- Human Rights Act
- United Nations Convention on the Rights of the Child

The Act was not designed specifically to protect children, but they are accorded the same rights as adults. This means they have a right to dignity, respect, and fairness in the way they are treated. The Human Rights Act means that the parents are also protected.

In addition to the Human Rights Act, the UK is also a signatory to the UN Convention on the Rights of the Child (UNCRC). This was drawn up in 1989 and gives children and young people under the age of 18 years their own special rights. There are five main strands to the convention:

1. It reinforces the importance of fundamental human dignity.
2. It highlights and defends the family's role in children's lives.
3. It seeks respect for children.
4. It endorses the principle of non-discrimination.
5. It establishes clear obligations for member countries to ensure that their legal framework is in line with the provisions of the convention.

The UNCRC is divided into articles, and below are some of the articles that might affect your dealing with children (Tessoni et al. 2007: 115):

- Article 2: the right to be protected from all forms of discrimination.
- Article 3: the best interest of the child to be the primary consideration in all actions concerning children.
- Article 12: a child's rights to express his or her views freely; a child's view to be given due weight in keeping with the child's age or maturity
- Article 13: a child's right to freedom of expression and exchange of information regardless of frontiers.

GILBERT GBEDAWO

- Article 28: a child's right to education with a view to achieving this right progressively on the basis of equal opportunities.

It is hoped that every parent and adult with responsibility of looking after children, whether at home or in a school setting, will rise to the task and promote the welfare and well-being of the children under their care so that children can attain educational excellence and become responsible adults in the future, capable of transforming the world and making it a better place for the next generation.

In England, the Secretary of State for Education has outlined in a speech delivered during the Sunday Times Festival of Education, Wellington College, Berkshire.

Let me include the whole speech delivered by the Secretary of State for Education today the 18th of June 2015 highlighting her vision for the next 5 years of education in England.

(https://www.gov.uk/government/speeches/nicky-morgan-discusses-the-future-of-education-in-england).

Good morning, and thank you Sir Anthony [Seldon, Master of Wellington College] for that very kind introduction.

It's a pleasure to speak here at Wellington College - a school that's gone from strength to strength over the last decade under your careful stewardship.

I'm sure staff and pupils, past and present, will look back on your time here with great fondness.

Certainly the ministerial team at the Department for Education have benefited from your wise and thoughtful advice, and long may that continue.

Today, of course, is the bicentenary of the Battle of Waterloo, marking the defeat of Napoleon and his army by the seventh coalition, with British troops being led by Arthur Wellesley, first Duke of Wellington, in whose honour this school is named.

A defining chapter in our history and a moment that helped make our nation great. A moment that showed British grit in the face of adversity. And our ability to stick it out, bounce back, keep calm and carry on. Shared values that bind us together as one nation.

When I think of those shared values, those shared experiences that make us proud to be British, I think of something I believe all of us here hold dear: our conviction that equality of opportunity is the cornerstone of a modern and enlightened society.

Education is at the heart of our governing philosophy

And education is the greatest way to level the playing field and give every child the chance to be all that they can be, and to reach their full potential.

This government has committed to deliver real social justice and in no arena more than education do we have such potential to realise it.

A good education is the key to the good life. A meaningful job. A sense of community and belonging. The skills to embrace the change and challenges of modern life in an increasingly global world.

Our plan

So I am proud of our drive over the past 5 years - our drive to ensure that every child is given the tools they need to develop and learn.

From phonics and times tables at primary schools, all the way through to new gold standard qualifications at 16 and 18, we need to ensure that young people master the basics in primary and develop that deep understanding in secondary.

GILBERT GBEDAWO

Because if our focus shifts, and if we lose sight of the fundamental knowledge and skills that form the heart of a rigorous curriculum, the people that lose out are the most disadvantaged.

It's those children for whom a good education matters most - children growing up in families where their parents and carers haven't had the same opportunities so many of us enjoy.

These young people are the people we cheat when we somehow pretend a core education doesn't matter. That false equivalents do the job just as well.

Which is why I announced earlier this week that every child starting in year 7 in September will be expected to study core academic subjects that make up the EBacc right up to GCSE.

Because one of my guiding principles - and I'm sure yours, too - is that every child, no matter their family circumstances, no matter where they're from or what their background is, can succeed if we give them the tools that allow them to achieve that success.

A rigorous academic curriculum must be central to that.

Creating the conditions for success

And if we're to have high expectations for every child, we have to create the right conditions for those high expectations, where a love for learning can flourish.

And we know that children need certain character traits to excel academically.

The kind of traits that should be embedded through a whole-school approach to character education, helping children and young people become decent, happy, well-balanced citizens.

I'm talking about exactly the kind of education that Anthony has championed for so long - I'm grateful for your research and support.

And, as you say, Anthony, academic attainment and exam success are just part of the story.

Building a strong character and a sense of moral purpose is part of the responsibility we have towards our children, our society and our nation.

Because if our schools don't nurture and develop these key traits, we run the risk of creating a generation who excel at passing exams, writing essays, absorbing information, but children without the skills they need to tackle the challenges that lie ahead and participate in society as active citizens, to make the right decisions and build their own moral framework.

I want to help our education system to nurture a generation that has the pioneering spirit and determination that's marked us out as a nation throughout history.

So as our academic reforms start to take root and restore our qualifications and examinations system to the gold standard it is supposed to enjoy, we have the perfect opportunity to look at the curriculum.

Things like:

- the character traits Doug Lemov wants to see all teachers foster in their classrooms - the skills that will help children remain on the right track as they embark on the next stage of their educational journey
- I want us to avoid the situation that was seen in the early stages of the American charter school system - highly motivated pupils, excellent results, but none of the skills needed to study independently and complete a degree
- the growth mindset, the ability to deal with set-backs, and the willingness to practice that Matthew Syed argues is essential to success

GILBERT GBEDAWO

Excellence

If I can sum up my ambition for the next 5 years it would be spreading the excellence in schools we've unlocked over the last 5 years everywhere across the country.

Our reforms have seen the unleashing of some truly excellent practice.

We've built on Andrew Adonis's fledgling academies programme to create a network of self-governing schools around the country - setting their own direction and giving parents choice.

Free schools like ARK Conway Academy, providing an outstanding and innovative education to some of the country's most disadvantaged children.

Or School 21, which I had the pleasure of visiting recently, with its continuous focus on character and integrity - attributes embedded into every aspect of school life.

Schools like these are the modern engines of social justice.

But - to be abundantly clear here - it's not the fact of being a free school or an academy that leads to this excellence.

Rather, it's what being an academy or a free school stands for.

Freeing up schools and governors to make decisions that are right for their pupils.

Greater competition and collaboration in the system. Encouraging local schools to learn from each other, share best practice and even partake in a bit of healthy rivalry!

The innovative approaches that come when you give teachers and school leaders freedom beyond the red tape and bureaucracy.

STEPS TOWARDS EDUCATIONAL EXCELLENCE

However, we have to acknowledge that excellence in the system is all too often confined to urban areas.

Pockets of under-performance persist in coastal and rural areas, and even in some of our leafy suburbs schools who have the capability to be really excellent are coasting along at 'just good enough'.

I know that changes take time to embed, that improvements don't happen all at once.

But consistent improvement and spreading excellence is what the next 5 years has to be about. And that's what the Education and Adoption Bill, which will receive its second reading next week focuses on.

The question I have asked myself, and the question I will continue to ask, is how I, as Secretary of State, can help to spread excellence throughout the school system, from the early years right through to sixth from, across the whole country? How can we ensure that by 2020 there aren't just 1 million more pupils in 'good' or 'outstanding' schools? How do we ensure we repeat this success?

We're at a new record high on the number of these 'good' or 'outstanding' schools, but this shouldn't stop us going even further.

And the reason I'm asking myself that is because a consistently excellent education system has to be at the heart of our commitment to govern as one nation.

Not just leveling

I've mentioned our aspirations for disadvantaged pupils, our conviction that central to social justice is closing the attainment gap that still persists.

But I want to do that by raising standards for everyone. Not working to the lowest common denominator.

GILBERT GBEDAWO

I don't want bright and driven kids from disadvantaged backgrounds to be content with average grades and average opportunities, simply because the gap has closed. I want a pupil premium that stretches them to the fullest degree.

That's why the historic focus on in-school gaps in attainment can't be our only focus - instead we should be ambitious for all.

Of course, it's right to expect that schools should be supporting all pupils to achieve a floor standard, but we can't afford to settle for the minimum.

Because true social justice means enabling the very brightest to jump from Bs to As, just as it does getting others from Ds to Cs.

Stability

I want to finish on a note of reassurance.

I don't want anyone to mistake stability for silence, to presume that education is no longer a priority for the government.

Education is a core part of this government's agenda for this Parliament.

The fact of the matter is that we now have to work with heads and teachers to make a reality of our new curriculum and qualifications.

The dust must settle; we must give schools the chance to seize the opportunities our reforms offer.

But, at the same time, I'm clear that the best schools should be able to extend their reach, to help more schools, more teachers and more pupils.

To borrow unashamedly from ASCL's blueprint for a self-improving school system, I want to use my time as Education Secretary to give schools and the profession the skills and capacity to improve, but

I want each and every one of you to take responsibility for that improvement. I want to unleash greatness in the system.

It's for all of us to ask the question: if it were possible for this head teacher, this school, this area to achieve that greatness, why would anyone else settle for less?

Thank you.

From: Department for Education The Rt Hon Nicky Morgan MP

This speech is vital as it sets the agenda for the next five years of education of all children in England. It is the responsibility of all parents and stakeholders in education to work together to ensure that all children receive an excellent education and grow into active citizens.

Permit me to reiterate the wisdom of Peter J. Daniel when he wrote:

> Success is for you because humanity itself strives always to win, to obtain, to overcome and to possess. Every new-born baby emphasises that hope and promise. Every new step taken by a young child illustrates success and accelerated the youngster on to greater achievement.
>
> Success is for you because God committed it to your development within the confines of the biblical charter. You were created, programmed and given opportunities to succeed and the responsibility is now yours.
>
> Success means total responsibility in my planning, my development, my achievement, my failures and my behaviour. These demonstrate a personal growth, a commitment to others and a respect for truth. This will lead us to our ultimate potential.

Make it your aim today to start developing an action plan to ensure that the children you are training and raising today go further. It is hoped that your children will exceed you spiritually, intellectually, morally, economically, politically, and financially, then we can be sure that you have succeeded in parenting and teaching them well. This, however, is no small task, but all things are possible to those who believe and have faith in God that the next generation can and should be better than the previous. These are the parents who build homes with wisdom and with the help of God. They partner with other like-minded individuals and institutions to raise outstanding children.

May your home, indeed, be that place where champions and leaders are trained and deployed to make the world a better place. God bless your home and those who live in it.

Gilbert's Family Pictures

Gilbert's dad- Gabriel

Gilbert and Obi

Gilbert's Graduation Pictures

Gilbert's graduation picture with the wife, Felicia.

Gilbert's Birthday Celebration with Mum at One.

Gilbert after thanksgiving church service

Gilbert with his friend Obi

Gilbert (the author) with his niece Patience (the bride), Bright (the groom) and Gilbert (the bride's dad).

Vanessa Odunsi

APPENDICES

Appendix A

Interview Questions for Students Attending Supplementary Schools

Introductions

1. State your name and date of birth.
2. How long have you been attending this supplementary school?
3. Please tell me the mainstream school you attend.

Student's View of the Supplementary School

1. Do you like supplementary school? What do you like best/least?
2. Why do you attend the supplementary school?
3. How different is the supplementary school to the school you attend?
4. How do you feel the supplementary school is contributing to your schoolwork?
5. Do you think the supplementary school will make any difference to your grades at GCSE, and if so, how?
6. What are the differences between teachers in the supplementary school and your school?

GILBERT GBEDAWO

Children's Supplementary School Experience (Exploring)

1. Who is supplementary school for? (Which children or community group do you think this supplementary school is for?)
2. What do you understand by the term 'your community'?
3. How often do you attend this supplementary school?
4. Are you taught in year, age, or ability groupings?
5. Which subjects or activities do you learn at this school? Why? What do you expect to gain from studying these lessons/activities?
6. Are the subjects and activities you learn different from what you are taught in your mainstream school? How? If the subjects/activities are the same as the subjects covered in the mainstream school, are they taught differently? How? Is there anything different about what you learn in your supplementary school compared to their mainstream school?
7. Are you given any homework? How much? And do you complete it?
8. How would you describe your supplementary school teachers? Are they different from the teachers in your mainstream school?
9. How would you describe the teaching support you receive?
10. Do you engage differently with your supplementary school lessons than your mainstream lessons? In what ways?
11. Are you better behaved at supplementary school compared to mainstream school? Why?
12. 1In what ways/areas have your supplementary school helped with your learning?
13. 1Are you encouraged to explore your identities (e.g. multilingual/faith/cultural)?
14. 1Does attending supplementary school help you to value your language/faith/culture more (depending on school provision)? Appreciate other cultures? Enjoy learning including other languages? Take any tests/exams?
15. 1What benefits do you think you get from attending supplementary school?

Connections between Supplementary and Mainstream Schooling (Further Probing)

1. Does attending supplementary school help with what you learn in mainstream school? (e.g. Are you more confident to ask questions or contribute to lesson discussions? Does it make you want to learn more, behave well, or take tests/examinations?
2. Are there any subjects/activities that you learn in your supplementary school which you would like to be taught in your mainstream school?
3. Do you have any examples of how you are supported in supplementary school which you think would work in your mainstream school and which would help you to learn?

Appendix B

Interview Questions for Parents/Carers of Children Attending Supplementary School

Parents Introduce Themselves

1. State your name.
2. Tell me about yourself and your family.
3. How many children do you have attending this supplementary school?
4. What are the ages of your children attending the supplementary school?
5. What is the name of the mainstream schools your children attend?

Supplementary School (Explore)

1. Why do you send your son/daughter to a supplementary school? (Advantages)
2. Why did you choose to send your son/daughter to this particular supplementary school?
3. How far does your son/daughter travel to attend this school?
4. How long has your son/daughter been attending this school?

Children's Supplementary School Experience (Further Probing)

1. Which subjects/activities does your son/daughter learn at this school?
2. Is your son/daughter given any homework? Do they complete it?
3. How would you describe your child's relationship with teachers and peers at the school?
4. How would you describe your child's behaviour at supplementary school?
5. How would you describe the teaching support your son/daughter receives?

STEPS TOWARDS EDUCATIONAL EXCELLENCE

6. How well does your child engage with their lessons in the supplementary school? Is this different from their mainstream school engagement?
7. In what way is the supplementary school helping your son/daughter's education?
8. Are there any other ways in which you think the supplementary school has benefited your son/daughter? Why?

Parental Experience of and Involvement in Supplementary School (Further Probing)

1. How are you involved in the supplementary school? Do you have any responsibilities at this school? What are they?
2. Do you contribute to the finances of the school (through fees/donations)?
3. How would you describe your relationship with the head teacher/teachers at this school? Is it different from your experience in your child's mainstream school?

Connections between Supplementary and Mainstream Schools (Further Probing)

1. Do you know if your child's supplementary school has any links/relationships with mainstream schools? If yes, how many?
2. Do you think it is important for supplementary schools to establish links/relationships with your children's mainstream schools? Do you think this would help raise your children's attainment and improve their understanding about themselves and their background? Would this help in developing better community understanding and relationships?
3. What do you think could be done to create links with mainstream schools?
4. Do you think your son or daughter's supplementary school attendance benefits his or her learning in mainstream school (e.g. increases confidence, encourages them to

learn, or enjoy learning more)? Does it help to improve their grades (e.g. in maths and English)?

5. What do you think supplementary school offers to your son/ daughter that they cannot get in their mainstream school? Is this something you would like to see offered in your child's mainstream school?

6. Finally, is there anything else that you would like to add that you think could help with this research?

Appendix C

Interview Questions for Teachers at Supplementary School

Introduction

Please introduce yourself by answering the following questions:

1. What is your name?
2. What subjects and year groups do you teach?
3. What motivated you to work in a supplementary school?
4. How long have you been teaching?
5. Do you teach in a mainstream school?
6. Do you have any teaching qualification and/or experience of teaching?
7. What trainings or preparations have you had to enhance your teaching in a supplementary school?
8. Do you have any other role apart from teaching? Briefly explain.

Probing Teaching and Learning

1. What specific learning needs do you aim to provide for during your lessons?
2. In your views, what does it take to teach in a supplementary school?
3. What are the challenges and constrains to your work in supplementary school.
4. What are some of the strategies that you use in your lessons, and how do you measure the effectiveness of those strategies?
5. Do you think that attending supplementary school can help improve African children's attainment in their mainstream school, and if so, how?
6. Do you think that attending supplementary school can affect your children's learning in their mainstream school? If so, how?
7. Do you think attending supplementary school helps African children to excel in their GCSE examinations? If so, how?

8. How would you compare your experience teaching in supplementary school with mainstream school? Are there any differences in terms of curriculum delivery, behaviour, interest, etc.?
9. Do you have any link with mainstream schools to enhance each other's work? If not, what are the barriers, and what can be done about them?
10. Do you think there are any differences between supplementary schools and mainstream school? If so, what are they?

Probing Parental Involvement

1. How do you involve parents/carers in their children's learning? Any strategies?
2. How crucial is parental involvement in promoting the children's educational attainment?
3. Please, is there anything else that you would like to add that you think could contribute to the outcome of this research?

Appendix D

Interview Questions for the Leadership/Management Team of the Supplementary School

Introduction

1. Please briefly describe yourself and your role in the supplementary school.
2. Can you describe more about the supplementary school, its aims, and its ethos?
3. What is the composition of students and teachers in your school?
4. What motivated you to set up or get involved in supplementary school?

Supplementary Schools and Their Impact on Migrant Children from Africa

1. To what extent do you think supplementary school attendance can affect your children's learning and attainment at GCSE in mainstream school? How?
2. Do you think there are any other benefits children get by attending supplementary schools?
3. In your view, what are you doing that mainstream schools are not already providing?
4. What has been your experience so far in terms of educational attainment of the students at GCSE?
5. How do you monitor the progress of the students who attend the supplementary school?
6. What, in your views, are the obstacles to the educational attainment of black migrant students?
7. What strategies do you put in place to address the underachievement of the students that attend your school?
8. How do you monitor and measure the success of your work?

Supplementary Schools and Mainstream Schools/Agencies

1. Does your school have any links with mainstream schools?
2. What do you think supplementary school offers to the students that mainstream school cannot give? Is this something you would like to see offered in the mainstream school?
3. What are the challenges with working with mainstream schools?
4. How are they funded? What are the challenges of running the school?
5. What are some barriers towards the smooth implementation of your project, and how do you overcome such challenges?

Supplementary School and Parental Involvement

1. How are parents involved in the supplementary school, and how important is this to your school?
2. Do parents contribute financially and/or as volunteers to the organisation? If so, to what extent?
3. What other services do you provide to the parents to help them support the learning experience of their children?
4. Finally, is there anything else you would like to add that you think could help with this research?

Appendix E

Interview Questions for LA Representative

1. Please briefly describe your work and what it entails?
2. How many supplementary schools are in your council, and why?
3. How would you describe the contributions of supplementary schools towards the education of migrant children in your borough/council?
4. How do you monitor and support the work of the supplementary schools in your council?
5. What criteria do you use to allocate resources to these schools?
6. What, in your views, are the obstacles to the educational attainment of black migrant students?
7. How are supplementary schools positioned to overcome black underachievement at GCSE?
8. How do you foster cooperation between mainstream and supplementary schools?
9. What is the way forward as far as supplementary schools are concerned?
10. 1What challenges do black parents face in their attempt to provide education for their children?
11. 1Which communities do supplementary schools in this LA serve?
12. How are supplementary schools funded? Are any of them funded by the LA? If so, what are the criteria for funding?
13. Do you think supplementary schools should be working with mainstream schools? If so, how do you facilitate this partnership?
14. What do you think is the future of supplementary schools' provision? Why?

REFERENCES

Abbot, D. (2007), 'Teachers are Failing Black Boys', in B. Richardson, ed., *Tell It Like It Is: How Our Schools Fail Black Children* (London: Bookmarks).

Acher, L. (2007), *Understanding Minority Ethnic Achievement: Race, Gender, Class, and 'Success'* (Oxon: Routledge).

Andrews, K. (2001), *Extra Learning: New Opportunities for the Out of School Hours* (London: Kogan Page).

Ball, S. J. (1981), *Beachside Comprehensive: A Case Study of Secondary Schooling* (Cambridge: Cambridge University Press).

Belfield, C. (2000), *Economic Principle for Education: Theory and Evidence* (Cheltenham: Edward Elgar Publishing Limited).

Bell, J. (2005), *Doing Your Research Project: A Guide for First-Time Researchers in Education, Health, and Social Science* (Berkshire: Open University Press).

Blair, M., and M. Cole (2006), 'Racism and Education: From Empire to New Labour', in M. Cole, ed., *Education, Equality, and Human Rights: Issues of Gender, 'Race', Sexuality, Disability and Social Class* (London: Routledge).

Blair, M. (2007), 'How Schools and Local Authorities Can Make the Difference to the Education of the Black Child', in B.

GILBERT GBEDAWO

Richardson, ed., *Tell It Like It Is: How Our Schools Fail Black Children* (London: Bookmarks).

Bourdieu, P. (2006), 'The Forms of Capital', in H. Lauder, P. Brown, J. Dillabough, and A. Halsey, eds, *Education, Globalisation, and Social Change* (Oxford: Oxford University Press).

Bricheno, P., and M. Thornton (2006), *Missing Men in Education* (London: Trentham Books).

Brown, W. (2007), 'The Future before Us', in B. Richardson, ed., *Tell It Like It Is: How Our Schools Fail Black Children* (London: Bookmarks).

Byfield, C. (2008), *Black Boys Can Make It: How They Overcome Obstacles to University in the UK and USA* (London: Trentham Books).

Cain, P. J., and A. G. Hopkins (2002), *British Imperialism: 1688–2000* (Essex: Pearson Education).

Checchi, D. (2007), *The Economics of Education: Human Capital, Family Background, and Inequality* (Cambridge: Cambridge University Press).

Coard, B. (1971), 'How the West Indian Child Is Made Educationally Subnormal in the British School System: The Scandal of the Black Child in Schools in Britain', in B. Richardson, ed., *Tell It Like It Is: How Our Schools Fail Black Children* (London: Bookmarks).

Coard, B. (2007), 'Thirty Years On: Where Do We Go from Here?', in B. Richardson, ed., *Tell It Like It Is: How Our Schools Fail Black Children* (London: Bookmarks).

Cole, M., and M. Blair (2006), 'Racism and Education: From Empire to New Labour', in M. Cole, ed., *Education, Equality, and Human Rights: Issues of Gender, 'Race', Sexuality, Disability, and Social Class* (New York: Routledge).

Council of Europe, ed. (1981), *The Education of Migrant Workers' Children: A Report of the European Contact Workshop Held at Dillingen, 14–18 April 1980 under the Auspices of the Council of Europe* (Lisse: Documentation Section of the Council of Europe).

Cox, D. (2007), 'A Parent's Choice', in B. Richardson, ed., *Tell It Like It Is: How Our Schools Fail Black Children* (London: Bookmarks).

Daniels, P. J. (1985), *How to Reach Your Life Goals* (Adelaide: World Centre for Entrepreneurial Studies).

DfES (2000), *Minority Ethnic Participation and Achievements in Education, Training, and Labour Market* (London: DfES).

DfES (2002), *Ethnic Minority Achievement Grant: Analysis of LEA Action Plan* (London: DfES).

DfES (2004), *Evaluation of Excellence in Cities/Ethnic Minority Achievement Grant (EIC/EMAG) Pilot Project* (London: DfES).

DfES (2005), *Minority Ethnic Pupils and Excellence in Cities: Final Report* (London: DfES).

DfES (2006), *Evaluation of Aiming High: African Caribbean Achievement Project* (London: DfES).

DfES (2008), *Minority Ethnic Pupils in Longitudinal Study of Young People in England: Extension Report on Performance in Public Examination at Age 16* (London: DfES).

DCSF (2010), *Impact of Supplementary Schools on Pupils' Attainment: An Investigation into What Factor Contribute to Educational Improvements* (London: DCSF).

DFE (2010), *A Review of the Longitudinal Study of Young People in England (LSYPE): Recommendations for a Second Cohort* (London: DFE).

GILBERT GBEDAWO

Fine, B., and F. Green (2000), 'Economics, Social Capital, and the Colonization of the Social Sciences', in S. Baron et al., eds, *Social Capital: Critical Perspectives* (Oxford: Oxford University Press).

Gillborn, D. (2008), *Racism and Education: A Coincidence or Conspiracy?* (London: Routledge).

Goodson, L., and J. Phillimore (2008), *New Migrants in the UK: Education, Training, and Employment* (London: Tretham Books).

Halpern, D. (2005), *Social Capital* (Cambridge: Polity Press).

Hanushek, E. (1994), *Making Schools Work: Improving Performance and Controlling Costs* (Washington DC: Brookings Institution).

Hatcher, R. (2006), 'Social Class and Schooling: Differentiation or Democracy?' in M. Cole, ed., *Education, Equality, and Human Rights: Issues of Gender, 'Race', Sexuality, Disability, and Social Class* (London: Routledge).

Hines, V. (1998), *How Black People Overcame Fifty Years of Repression in Britain: 1945–1995* (London: Zulu Publication).

HM Treasury (2008), *Social Bridges II: The Importance of Human Capital for Growth and Social Inclusion* (London: HM Treasury).

Issa, T. and C. Williams (2009), *Realising Potential: Complementary Schools in the UK* (Staffordshire: Trentham Books).

Jones, V. A. (1986), *We Are Our Own Educators! Josina Machel: From Supplementary to Black Complementary School* (London: Karia Press).

Lauglo, J. (2000), 'Social Capital Triumphing Class and Cultural Capital? Engagement with School among Immigrant

Youth', in S. Baron et al., eds, *Social Capital: Critical Perspectives* (Oxford: Oxford University Press).

Kunjufu, J. (1990), *Countering the Conspiracy to Destroy Black Boys*, vol. 3 (Illinois: Tenth Printing).

Leary, J. D. (2005), *Post-Traumatic Slave Syndrome: America's Legacy of Enduring Injury and Healing* (Oregon: Uptone Press).

Lentin, A. (2008), 'Racism, Anti-Racism and the Western State', in G. Delanty et al., eds, *Identity, Belonging, and Migration* (Liverpool: Liverpool University Press).

Livingstone, D. W. (1997), 'Living in the Credential Gap: Responses to Underemployment and Underqualification', in A. Duffy et al., eds, *Good Jobs, Bad Jobs, No Jobs: The Transformation of Work in the 21st Century* (Toronto: Harcourt Brace).

Livingstone, D. W. (1997), 'The Limits of Human Capital Theory: Expanding Knowledge, Informal Learning, and Underemployment', in A. Duffy et al., eds, *Good Jobs, Bad Jobs, No Jobs: The Transformation of Work in the 21st Century* (Toronto: Harcourt Brace).

Mirza, H. S. (2007), 'The More Things Change, the More They Stay the Same: Assessing Black Underachievement 35 Years On', in B. Richardson, ed., *Tell It Like It Is: How Our Schools Fail Black Children* (London: Bookmarks).

Muir, H. (2007), 'We Need Allies to Win These Battles: We Should Heed This Prison-Cell Warning of the Perils of Trying to Beat Equality Alone', in E. Prokopiou and T. Cline, eds, *Constructing Cultural and Academic Identities in Community Schools: A Socio-Cultural and Dialogical Approach* (Staffordshire: Trentham Books).

Munn, P. (2000), 'Social Capital, Schools, and Exclusions', in S. Baron et al., eds, *Social Capital: Critical Perspectives* (Oxford: Oxford University Press).

OECD (2010), *Closing the Gap for Immigrant Students: Policies, Practice, and Performance* (Paris: OECD).

Phillimore, J., and L. Goodson (2008), *New Migrants in the UK: Education, Training, and Employment* (Staffordshire: Trentham Books).

Pilkington, A. (2003), *Racial Disadvantage and Ethnic Diversity in Britain* (New York: Palgrave Macmillan).

Reed, H., and E. Loughran, eds. (1984), *Beyond Schools: Education for Economic, Social, and Personal Development* (Amherst: University of Massachusetts).

Reynolds, G. (2008), *The Impacts and Experiences of Migrant Children in UK Secondary Schools Working Paper No. 47* (Sussex: University of Sussex).

Richardson, B., ed. (2007), *Tell It Like It Is: How Our Schools Fail Black Children* (London: Bookmarks).

Schuller, T., et al. (2000), 'Social Capital: A Review and Critique', in S. Baron et al., ed., *Social Capital: Critical Perspectives* (Oxford: Oxford University Press).

Simon, D. (2007), 'Education of All the Black: The Supplementary School Movement', in B. Richardson, ed., *Tell It Like It Is: How Our Schools Fail Black Children* (London: Bookmarks).

Tassoni, P., K. Beith, K. Bulman, and H. Eldridge (2007), *Child Care and Education* (Oxford: Heinemann).

Tomlinson, S. (2007), 'A Tribute to Bernard Coard', in B. Richardson, ed., *Tell It Like It Is: How Our Schools Fail Black Children* (London: Bookmarks).

Yin, R. (2009), *Case Study Research: Design and Methods* (London: Sage).

INDEX

A

Abraham (patriarch)   113-15, 126-7, 130

Adam (first man)   132

Africa   1, 3-4, 6-8, 11-12, 15-19, 23, 27, 33, 38, 50-1, 59, 63-4, 93, 124-5, 185

African Caribbean   9, 11-12, 15-17, 19, 23, 193

Aiming High   17, 24, 193

anonymity   35, 43

Asians   xiv, 6, 9, 11, 18, 50-1

autodidacticism   73

B

Bangladeshi   6-7, 9

blacks   xiii, xvii, 3-4, 6-21, 25, 31, 38, 50-3, 55, 58, 60, 63-4, 66-7, 189, 191-6

C

charity   xiv, 103-4

Chinese   7, 9, 16, 24, 50-1, 85

cultural differences   3, 12

D

DCSF (Department for Children Schools and Families)   xv, 22, 24-5, 55, 193

DFE (Department for Education)   xv, 16-17, 24, 193

DfES (Department for Education and Schools)   xv, 16-17, 24, 193

E

education   73

educational system   1, 57, 154-5

EEC (European Economic Community)   23

GILBERT GBEDAWO

EiC (Excellence in Cities) 8, 15, 193
ethnic groups 5-7, 9-11, 14-16, 26,
   31, 47, 51
Eve (first woman) 132
examinations 49, 61, 65, 78, 83, 97

G

gap, attainment 5, 9, 15, 17, 44, 62
GCSE (General Certificate of
   Secondary Education) 3, 6-7,
   10-11, 16, 18, 45-6, 61, 68, 90-1,
   179, 185, 187, 189

H

Hagar (handmaid of Sarah) 114-16
HCT (human capital theory) xv, 27-
   8, 44-5, 49-50, 61, 195
heritage 53-4, 140, 144
Human Rights Act 157

I

identity 52-4, 63-5, 180, 195
ignorance 75
Indians 6, 50-1
interviews 27, 32-43, 45, 48-9, 51,
   55, 57-8, 65, 90, 92, 94
investment 28, 49, 51, 72, 94, 101,
   114
Ishmael (son of Hagar) 116-17

K

KICC (Kingsway International
   Christian Centre) xiv-xv
knowledge xi, xiii, 8, 26-8, 55, 58,
   69-73, 76-8, 81, 84, 100, 103,
   129-33, 143-5, 154-5

L

languages 31, 58, 90, 124, 180
LEA (local education authority) 7,
   9, 16, 193

M

mainstream schools xvii, 3-4, 11, 21,
   33, 40, 44-5, 47-9, 54-9, 64-7, 89,
   179-89
mentors 16, 79-81, 99-100, 109, 147
migrants 1-2, 4, 11, 15, 19, 21, 26,
   31, 33, 38, 41, 44, 46, 60-1, 64-6
migration 1, 8, 36, 195
minority xvii, 5-7, 15-16, 22-4, 31, 47,
   50-1
motivation 21, 25-6, 51, 65, 86-7,
   106, 129, 148

N

Nigeria 101
NRC (National Resource Centre)
   22, 24, 64

STEPS TOWARDS EDUCATIONAL EXCELLENCE

O

Odunsi, Vanessa 89
OECD (Organisation for Economic Co-Operation and Development) xv, 8, 14-15, 29, 196
outstanding students 77, 80, 82, 86, 88

P

parenthood 72, 105
parents, role of 3, 44, 57, 60, 103
poverty 8, 125, 133
prayer xiii-xiv, 72, 76, 79, 87, 103, 109, 112, 126-7, 130-1, 150

R

racism 18, 21, 36, 67, 93, 191-2, 194-5

S

Sarah (wife of Abraham) 113-14
SCT (social capital theory) xv, 27, 29, 44, 51, 55, 61
secondary schools xvii, 1-4, 10, 15, 17-20, 22, 31, 38, 41, 44, 55, 66, 94, 196
self-esteem xvii, 26, 153
students, role of 68
SWOT analysis 108-9

T

teachers xiv, xviii, 12-13, 21, 35-6, 45, 52-6, 58-61, 66-7, 71-2, 80, 97, 99-101, 179-80, 182-3
Traveller of Irish heritage 9

U

UNCRC (UN Convention on the Rights of the Child) 157
underachievement 13, 17, 19, 21, 25, 56, 64, 187
unemployment 50
unity 123, 125, 147
university 45-6, 91, 93-4, 110, 133, 192

W

whites xvii, 6-12, 15-16, 18-19, 25-6, 47, 50-1, 58, 62, 64

Y

YLN (Youth Learning Network) xv, 45, 51, 59

Lightning Source UK Ltd.
Milton Keynes UK
UKOW04n1035131015

260434UK00001B/8/P